Emotional 911:

For Parents

First Aid for Your Child's
Emotional Scrapes and Scars

Laura Sonderegger

Emotional 911: For Parents
© 2018 Laura Sonderegger
www.laurasond.com

Published by Get Real Healing

For Katie,
who brings light, love and laughter
to all our lives.

Table of Contents

Resources

Acknowledgements:

This book would never have happened without the encouragement from, and accountability to, dear friends and family – especially Kiera Schvaneveldt.

I am indebted to Carolyn Casey, Stacey Lytle, Kylee Wiscombe, Kayla Rich, Megan Bryant, Wendy Alexandre, MerriDee Copeland, and the rest of my Zena Tribe.

I am grateful to Renee Settle for her "12-Minutes-A-Day" workbook that helped me take my first, tentative baby steps into writing (www.reneesettle.com).

Special thanks to my editors: Jerusha Smith, Molly Davenport, and Lauri Fredrickson.

And finally, love and appreciation to my incredible husband, Clayn, who validates me every single day and holds my hand along our way!

Introduction

It's difficult to pinpoint the precise moment your world turns upside-down or inside-out. When a clock breaks, you know the exact time with the hands frozen in place, but our lives are different. Life ticks regularly along until the day it doesn't . . . the day of the "incident," "diagnosis," or "awareness."

One day, I was tardy picking up my fourth-grade daughter after school. I was delayed by something unremarkable--a slow checkout line, or perhaps congested traffic--and all of the other kids were gone when I arrived. The crossing guard had walked Katie up the long driveway to the school office where she sat, waiting for me. Breathlessly rushing in, I apologized to the staff and my tearful daughter, and then we went home. Little did I know that this seemingly simple incident would eventually snowball into an all-consuming avalanche.

At first, it looked like Katie was just overreacting. Worrying that I might forget again to pick her up from school, each morning began with a tear-filled battle. Soon, Katie was calling me several times each day from school, begging to come home, or for reassurance that I would remember to pick her up at the end of school.

Any change in the normal routine of the school day would create a complete emotional meltdown with tears and anxiety. She stopped going to friends' houses after school or on weekends, and became reclusive. Weeks, and then months passed, with my daughter's anxiety spilling over into every area of our lives. Clearly, we were in over our heads . . . drowning.

Even though I'm a strong swimmer, there was no way to keep my head constantly above water while the weight of my child's pain pulled me under. Helplessness, guilt, and worry washed over me like never-ending ocean waves.

Treading water, while trying to keep my daughter afloat, left me exhausted and on the verge of collapse. I felt lost and alone, desperately grasping for any individual, resource, or tool that might hold me up for one more day . . . or even one more hour.

As a parent, we suffer twice: once for our child and once for ourselves. When my daughter began struggling with anxiety, her bad days became my bad days; her drama became my drama; her pain became mine. While my daughter was hurting, I was hurting, and I had no idea where to find help. I felt helpless to relieve either her suffering or mine.

Feeling overwhelmed and confused, I desperately wished for crisis tools to bring immediate relief, while we also worked to resolve the root issues. I was in desperate need of support and tools to give aid *RIGHT THEN*!

My story could be your story; perhaps just a different variety, like brands of cereal. While your burden may come in a different size or package, it may contain similar ingredients: fear, frustration, overwhelm, discouragement, despair, and helplessness.

Are you struggling with a similar circumstance? Do you have a child grappling with anxiety, depression, mental illness, or other challenges, whether diagnosed or suspected? Has an incident of abuse, harm, or bullying affected your child? Searching for solutions, waiting months for medical or counseling appointments, and feeling beaten down from the daily battle, you may find yourself losing heart and hope.

You could be worrying about a child who doesn't seem to fit in, or who is being bullied. Your child might be aching with emotional pain from divorce, relocation, or other loss.

You might have a child struggling with depression, anxiety, or one of the many forms of mental illness. There could be physical health problems or challenges related to ADD/ADHD, or Autism Spectrum Disorder.

Or, maybe you're just trying to figure out how to connect with your healthy child now, so that when challenges arise, you will have developed emotional resilience habits to successfully navigate the storm.

The truth is that in every scary, vulnerable, painful, uncomfortable, life-altering moment in my life, all I've wanted is someone to hold my hand. On days when there was no one to hold my hand, God gave me the needed hope to believe I would be guided to know what to do, and find better days ahead.

No matter the need, you are not alone! Nor were you meant to navigate the twists and turns of life on your own. If you are seeking support and guidance out of the quicksand-sinking heaviness of a hurting child, the answers and I are here.

This book was written for you, if you:

- feel engulfed with the present emotional needs and demands of your child
- require resources to remedy previous emotionally-damaging incidents or situations experienced by your child
- desire healthy attachment and closer communication with your child
- want to foster confidence, emotional resilience, and a growth mindset in your child
- yearn to improve your parenting skills and restore balance to your life

If you are seeking emotional first aid tools you can use, **whether in crisis or everyday parenting**, I will hold your hand and show you how to find help, hope, and happiness again.

Lifelines

"A hero is an ordinary individual who
finds strength to persevere and endure
in spite of overwhelming obstacles."
– Christopher Reeve

As first responders, parents are always on duty. We are usually the first to arrive and offer aid. Our child may have a crisis at any hour, day or night. Sometimes, we treat a singular incident, but more often the issue involved is situational, possibly dragging on for weeks, months, or even years.

Our first instinct as humans is to sacrifice ourselves to save a loved one who is hurting or in danger. Seeing our floundering child, and heedless of the hazards, we blindly dive to the rescue.

Fully immersed, with our child desperately clinging to us, we no longer have the capacity to keep ourselves - and our child - above water. It feels as if our child pushes off us to propel themselves above water, while we sink deeper and deeper below the surface. Once in the water, we often get sucked into a whirlpool of pain, shame or blame.

**First aid becomes useless if you can't
safely perform it without injuring yourself.**

As a parent, solely attempting to save a child who is struggling can put *us* in harm's way. Without the right skills, tools, and equipment, we can quickly find ourselves becoming helpless right along with our child.

Stress, anxiety, excessive worrying, irrational fears, depression, sleep disruption and physical problems are not just experienced by a child in crisis, but often by parents, too. Remember, we can't take care of others if we don't take care of ourselves.

Continual care-giving can take a toll on *our* physical, mental, and emotional strength.

Living in Idaho near some of the world's best whitewater rafting, I have observed how experienced river-rafting guides rescue someone who has fallen into the water:

- **The guide stays in the boat.** Using a special rescue bag, a lifeline is thrown to the person who is in trouble from the ideal position of being able to give the most help. This allows the guide to pull the struggling individual back toward the safety of the boat, while keeping control of the craft.

- **The guide is equipped** with an extra-buoyant life jacket designed to support not just their weight, but the extra burden of someone else's weight should the guide have to momentarily leave the safety of the boat, or get pulled into the water.

Even while my child's challenges threatened to pull me under, hope was like a life vest keeping me afloat. Hope allowed me to discover the world of emotional healing, and develop buoyant emotional first aid tools that can bring immediate support and relief.

If you find yourself out of the boat and floundering in the water, grab a lifeline back to safety.

Lifeline Definition:

1) *a rope or line used for life-saving, typically one thrown to rescue someone in difficulties in the water.*

2) *a thing on which someone or something depends, or which provides a means of escape from a difficult situation.*

Lifeline One: "Everything is going to be okay."

One of the primary steps of first aid is to make sure the person in crisis is breathing. Take a second, breathe deeply, and embrace this phrase: "Everything is going to be okay."

I can't explain why those six words bring such relief. Perhaps it's because deep down, you know that you are a survivor. No matter how bad things have been, how hard things are right now, or how much further you must go, you will make it. You are not alone, and answers will come. There are good days ahead, always!

Lifeline Two: Put on your own oxygen mask first.

As part of airplane safety, passengers are told, "In the event of an emergency, put on your own oxygen mask *before* helping those around you." This important rule ensures survival in real life as well. When placing the needs of others before our own, especially in times of crisis, it is easy to become stressed, depleted, and even experience personal health challenges.

How do you recharge?

When a cell phone crashes, the computer freezes, or the cable connection circles, the first remedy to try is powering down the device and restarting it. Almost everything works better after being unplugged for a few minutes.

The same can be said for you. You won't be able to love, serve, strengthen, and support if you don't maintain your own health. Give yourself permission to carve out a few minutes for self-care each day.

Recharging your physical and emotional batteries can look like many things: regular exercise, healthy diet, increased sleep, and finding things that spark joy for you. It means spending time (even just ten minutes), *EVERY SINGLE DAY* on a renewal activity.

Self-Care Suggestions:

- Listen to uplifting music (whether lying down with your eyes closed, or having your own private, cut-loose dance party).
- Get outside (a few minutes of sunshine works wonders).

- Sit quietly (even if you must lock yourself in the pantry, the bedroom closet, or the bathroom).
- Go animal (pet the cat, feed the ducks, or walk the dog).
- Choose inspirational quotes to print or pin where you can see them (try making a Pinterest board by categories with pins that make you laugh, re-center your faith, or refocus your priorities).
- Take a walk around the block (or stride back and forth in front of your own home while the kiddos peer out the window making faces at you).
- Breathe deeply while holding a few yoga poses (yes, even the "Corpse Pose" counts).

- Spend some time in prayer (not just pouring out your heart to God, but also listening for personal guidance).
- Smell a favorite, mood-boosting essential oil (dispense on your body's pulse points, or diffuse into a room).
- Read the comics – whether in a newspaper, a book, or online (*Calvin and Hobbs,* as well as *Zits,* are two of my favorites).

- Ponder or add to a "bucket list" of joy-bringers (having something to look forward to releases happiness hormones).
- Read from an inspiring book (a paragraph, page, or chapter).
- Write a few lines in a journal (whether venting frustrations, or naming blessings).
- Watch a funny YouTube video (laughter is a great stress-reliever; find what makes you laugh out loud).

Tip: Studies shows that simply viewing cat videos can boost energy levels and increase feelings of happiness.

- Get organized. (Working through the clutter in your life eliminates energy drains. Start by cleaning one drawer, cupboard, or closet at a time.)
- Practice visualizations. (Focus on imagining your own "secret garden," a place you would love to visit, or draw from memories of a real "happy place" from your past. Consider playing background music with soothing nature sounds, or listen to a guided meditation.)

- Phone a supportive friend (making sure to "lead with what you need"). See the following box for how-to tips.

How to "Lead With What You Need."

When we look to others for support during precious self-care minutes, it is essential that time be about you. I'm not suggesting that the universe should revolve around you every day, or that you shouldn't have a balance of giving and taking in relationships.

However, I have learned *not* to ask how my friend or family member is doing when I truly feel empty or need encouragement. Instead, I remind myself to "lead with what I need."

State your purpose for the call or conversation with clear intent.

Use phrases such as:

- "I'm really struggling today; I was hoping you had five minutes to let me vent."
- "I'm calling because I need you to remind me that everything is going to be okay."
- "I'm hoping you have a few minutes to listen and give me some advice."
- "I've locked myself in the pantry and just need to hear a friendly voice."
- "Would you be available to . . . run to the store/watch my kids for an hour/bring me a diet Dr. Pepper sometime today?"

Self-care shows up in other conversations. When we say "yes" to someone else, we have to evaluate if that's a "no" to ourselves. While you may not be advertising to the world that you are in "Survival Mode," you can create personal boundaries of space and time.

A useful phrase to avoid accepting an assignment or invitation, without explanation, is simply: "That's not going to work for me." You can add qualifiers, such as, "That's not going to work for me today/this week/right now." Should people press for details, simply repeat the same phrase until they clue-in to the fact that *it is none of their business* why it's not going to work for you.

Self-care *IS*
taking care of others!

By strapping on your own oxygen mask first, you ensure that you have the life-saving vitality to love, serve, and give from a position of strength rather than one of weakness.

Lifeline three: Don't paddle alone.

 It's not uncommon to feel like our child's struggle is a family secret that can't be shared with others. Sometimes, shame plays out in our heads and makes us afraid to look like a parenting failure. Other times, we feel pressure to prove (*to whom?*) that we are strong enough to solve problems on our own.

Courage doesn't always come from within.
Sometimes courage comes
from the support we feel from others.

One of my favorite YouTube videos shows a bus stop in Montreal, Canada, outfitted with heaters which can only be powered by human connection. Part of an advertising campaign for Duracell, a banner reads: "In Canada, we have cold winters, but we also have each other" (*Duracell Canada Moments of Warmth surprise bus shelter*, 2015).

By placing palms against sensors on opposite walls and then holding hands, two or more people can create a human chain to complete the circuit. This triggers heat from the vents in the shelter's ceiling.

Working together, we can make
an unbearable situation bearable.

There is no shame in needing or asking for support. As you do, you will be surprised at how many others have struggled, or are currently struggling, with similar concerns.

Join or start a support group with other parents. Schedule a meeting with your child's school teacher, counselor, and/or administrator to get others on your team. Find supportive friends and encourage your child to do the same. Ask extended family to step in so you can take a break and get your head above water.

Rowing Together

Parenting is like putting two first time paddlers in a canoe. Unless you learn how to row together, you may find yourself frustrating--spending a lot of energy without getting anywhere.

Navigating the emotional and physical currents of parenting is not without hazards. Dr. John Gottman, relationship expert and author, calls marriage "a cross-cultural experience," with each spouse bringing unique culture from their own upbringing.

Differences in parenting styles aren't usually revealed until difficulties arise. Children can sense when parents are not in sync and will rock the boat, dividing attention and undermining authority.

Here are a few tips to get you paddling together:

- Study "maps" to determine where you're headed as a family. Share ideas from parenting books (like this one), blogs, or podcasts to create a united front when responding to your child's choices and needs.
- Identify core values and describe areas you may be willing to compromise (such as bedtimes, chores, grades, sports, holidays, etc.).
- Define discipline, family rules and reasonable consequences when things are calm.
- Tackle high-stress situations as a team. Discuss common behavior concerns you may be noticing and create a plan of action together.

- Empathize with your child but support your spouse. Provide back up when one parent disciplines a child (as long as it's not abusive). If you don't agree, discuss privately and readdress later with your child should both parents approve an alternative solution.
- Ask for what you need. Be sure to use "I" messages ("I feel overwhelmed") vs. "you" judgments ("You never help").

Raising children is a long ride so try to keep things in perspective. Be flexible and strive to balance the total stress load to keep from capsizing. With a little communication, cooperation and collaboration you'll soon create a synchronized rhythm of successful parenting.

Remember, it is much easier to navigate through the whitewater rapids of life when you have other paddlers in your boat, and a seasoned guide, like me, who has been down the river before. Together, we will chart a course for emotional well-being for you and your loved ones.

How to Use This Book

As a parent, I know what it feels like to be in crisis, desperate for a "quick fix" to help a child who is hurting. I wish it was possible to provide an index where you could look up your child's specific challenge, and flip to a page for the answer. This book does not offer that format, since each child, parent and situation is unique. Still, the remedy for almost every emotional need is based on core principles which, once understood, prepare you to apply the suggested practices.

Healing goes deeper than curing.

Most doctors offer cures--external remedies such as medications or procedures--to mask or eliminate symptoms without resolving the root issue. In contrast, healing addresses the causal factors, such as disturbing events or unmet needs, which contributed to the symptoms in the first place.

This book supplies the principles (the "what") and practices (the "how") to equip parents with the emotional first aid skills, tools, and resources to address a child's ever-changing emotional needs, providing lasting healing.

Divided into 3 parts, this guidebook breathes new life into your parenting capacity with Emotional CPR.

C = Care

Chapters 1-8: Be aware and be there. Learn to listen for cues of emotional distress. Once detected, be ready to apply emotional first aid procedures designed to offer immediate help for everyday distress and drama. The Validation Hero Recipe provides immediate relief for almost every situation.

P = Prepare

Chapters 9-12: Discover intentional, immunizing activities designed to help a child develop resilience, flexibility and grit. For some issues, a child needs to be taught to *cope* with a situation or diagnosis. In other cases, it's imperative to *clear* emotional pain to prevent a distressing event from developing into a greater crisis, or producing lasting damage.

R = Repair

Chapters 13-18: Furnishing tools for treating advanced needs and healing past trauma, the 3-step Emotional 911 Sequence will help you detect the (*often hidden*) root cause of a child's mental or physical challenges. This procedure supplies specific direction for transforming negative emotions and beliefs into positive, powerful energy.

No matter what has happened or is happening, emotional first aid has the capacity to change what an experience means to our child. Therein lies the source of real healing.

Part I: CARE

Chapter 1: Emotional First Aid

"Caring for the mind is as important and
crucial as caring for the body. In fact, one
cannot be healthy without the other."
— Sid Garza-Hillman

Accidents happen. Disasters occur. Emergencies strike. Not knowing when these things could happen, we want to be prepared.

First aid helps us cope with a crisis. It involves the process of assessing and addressing the needs of someone who has been injured to quickly determine the correct course of treatment.

The same method is required for treating emotional injury or pain. In addition to the normal stash of Band-Aids, balms and painkillers, we must prepare for emotional emergencies with a supply of emotional first aid solutions.

**While addressing physical injury is critical,
it may be even more crucial to attend
to pain we can't see on the outside.**

As much as we want to protect our child from experiencing trouble or trauma, life happens. It's like driving a car down the road when a rock suddenly flips up from a passing car, smacking the windshield. Sometimes the stone impacts the window with a whacking sound which startles or scares you, but leaves no lasting blemish.

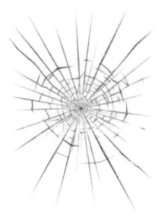

On occasion, a seemingly small pebble may collide with sufficient force making a visible starburst mark. Even the most careful or defensive driving can't prevent the sudden damage.

Left untreated, the web-shaped crack crawls across the window, limiting or completely blocking your ability to see, until repaired.

Similarly, as parents, we can't prevent life from impacting our child. How drama or trauma affect a child's physical or emotional state depends primarily on how a child interprets the event, and the meaning assigned to it.

Some emotionally-charged incidents might startle or scare, but bounce off and are forgotten. Other jolts may land forcefully, leaving an emotional fracture requiring repair.

Left unacknowledged, this event can create a lasting emotional scar, or develop into a limiting belief which blocks our child's ability to feel safe, loved, or see the world clearly, until remedied.

Interactions with peers and others, whether virtual or in person, inevitably produce painful blows and bumps on our child's psyche. Just as we would address a skinned knee, we must be prepared to respond to our child's emotional scrapes.

When experiencing physical or psychological trauma, we want our child to bounce back instead of break.

To prevent a window from breaking to bits upon impact, car windshields are manufactured with layers of special glass. As parents, our emotional first aid aptitude creates layers of safety, shielding our child from potentially shattering clashes. Should emotional injury strike, our empathetic presence provides needed strength and structure to facilitate solutions which repair the damage.

Yet, when the need exceeds our abilities, it's time to dial 9-1-1, the universal number for urgent assistance. Now you can access Emotional 911 expertise, offering immediate emotional first aid for:

- bullying or abuse
- anxiety, depression, or aggression
- divorce or family fallout
- social, school, or sports stress
- mental health challenges (either diagnosed or suspected)

Whether addressing a child's everyday emotional scrapes, bumps and bruises, treating prior trauma scars, or seeking support for long-term situations, this book supplies the life-saving skills of Emotional 911.

Note: Emotional first aid may not be the only action needed for every difficult situation. Diagnosis and treatment might be required at another point on the continuum of care. However, a quick response to emotional pain increases the speed of recovery. Emotional first aid provides a welcome practice for addressing initial distress and/or treating suppressed trauma.

Chapter 2: Good Thing You're So Tough

"Life is rough so you gotta be tough."
– Johnny Cash

At a recent girls' camp, one fourteen-year-old young woman was pointing out multiple mosquito bites on her body. While irritating, these itchy bumps were neither life-threatening nor long-lasting. Acknowledging her annoyance, I responded with our family mantra, "Good thing you're so tough!" Giving me a wry smile, she returned her focus to the activity in progress.

Around the world, toughness and bravery are praised. Did you know that in some areas of Japan, elementary-school children are forced to dress in tee-shirts and shorts, even in winter? *Gaman,* or "enduring something difficult," is an esteemed virtue by the Japanese.

The United States, and many European cultures, also praise toughness. Boys are often told to "man up" by participating in traditionally macho activities, such as hunting and sports, or to "walk it off" when they receive an injury. When hurt or worried, a boy who expresses emotional fears with tears risks ridicule and rejection by teammates, parents, or others.

Seeking peer approval, boys often engage in risky behavior to prove their manhood. (Think of the well-known words, "Hey, watch this!" which means, "I'm about to do something extremely risky and stupid.")

While gender bias allows girls to be more emotionally expressive than boys, societal expectations pressure girls to show more compassion, empathy,

and be happy all of the time.

These demands often lead girls to internalize negative emotions such as sadness, fear, anxiety, guilt, and shame. In addition, evidence indicates women have a negativity-recall bias, which means females typically remember mistakes more than males.

Whether trying to prove toughness or wrestling with regrets, a pattern of suppressing emotions can lead to depression, anxiety, or even suicidal thoughts.

An old-school believer in the saying, "If you baby a child they will stay a baby" my husband encouraged toughness with our children. Any time a child would get hurt or come crying, he would say, "Good thing you're so tough." This phrase can be a great way to sort out whether a child is simply seeking validation, or genuinely requires aid.

While the concept of encouraging toughness works for minor mishaps, what about the times when you're hurting too much to be tough?

When our oldest son, Josh, was in fourth grade, my husband played on a city-league baseball team. One night, while the men were playing baseball on one field, several of our kids were fooling around on a nearby field that was not in use. Sometime during the game, one of the boys came running over and said our son had fallen and was "hurt bad." The game in progress abruptly stopped, and several adults - including myself and my husband - ran to the adjacent field.

Upon arrival, we found our son lying semi-conscious on the grass near third base. We could see the obvious dips and bows of broken bones in both arms.

Confused as to how he could have been hurt, we asked what had happened. One of the boys confessed that they had been "sword fighting" with sticks on top of a partially-submerged dugout. Josh had retreated to the edge where he fell, eight feet onto the concrete steps below. He had somehow managed to stand and walk up the steps before collapsing on the field. Unbeknownst to us at the time, the impact to the right side of his skull hitting the steps below caused a basilar skull fracture.

The first thing his dad said was, "Just give him a minute and he'll get up." Looking back, his dad realizes that was not the best response. Clearly, Josh couldn't "tough" himself out of this situation. An ambulance was called, and Josh was taken to the local children's hospital, where he spent several days in the ICU, and then several weeks with both arms in casts.

What causes us to not want to acknowledge genuine wounds, injuries, and pain? Does acknowledging physical hurt create a wimpy child?

How about psychological pain? In cases of legitimate mental illnesses, such as Bipolar Disorder, general anxiety, depressive or Obsessive-Compulsive Disorders, telling the child to "be happy" or to "control your thoughts" is not only ineffective, but cruel.

When a child is told to "toughen up," what lasting harm might be created?

 Just like a pebble splashing into a pond, there is a ripple-effect generated when physical or emotional pain is invalidated or belittled (Kircher-Morris, 2015).

Minutes later:

Our child feels shamed or betrayed by their emotions. Instead of feeling safe speaking up, our child feels foolish or weak for bringing up an issue or difficulty. Without validation, our child is taught to disconnect from his or her feelings, and hide fear, sadness, or vulnerability. Our child may also disconnect from the parent, coach, teacher, or person who down-played his or her pain, seeming not to care.

Months later:

When not allowed to feel all of his or her emotions, our child may begin to act out. Gender may influence how unexpressed emotions manifest themselves. During childhood, boys are more likely to have behavior problems, such as defiance, impulsivity and aggression, which are often associated with high levels of anger (Cole, 1994). With a naturally shorter fuse, boys might *explode* at teachers, classmates, siblings or parents.

As teens, girls are more likely than boys to have symptoms of sadness and fear (Hankin). Girls may *implode* into melancholy, depression, or anxiety.

Having been taught to dismiss, suppress, or ignore feelings in the past, our child may resist sharing feelings now, should we try to discuss an uncomfortable or difficult situation.

Years Later:

Now a teenager or young adult, our child may have trouble showing empathy toward the emotions of others, because he or she expects others to "be tough" when challenges arise. Whenever someone gets hurt, our friend, Paul Glenn, quips, "Casualties happen." Yet truly, lack of the ability to relate to another's suffering can affect friendships, romantic relationships, and future parenting.

In addition, our child may have become emotionally numb to *any* feelings-- positive or negative--since feelings work on an "all-or-nothing" switch. Seeking to suppress the negative, he or she can lose the ability to feel the positive emotions as well.

37

Accumulating evidence suggests that when a person is either limited in the range of emotions expressed, or encouraged to express certain emotions at the exclusion of others, there is a **greater likelihood of emotions manifesting as physical problems, and a higher risk for developing psychological issues** (Babbel, 2010).

Josey grew up on a farm, and was expected to do a man's work from the time she was a little girl. As young as eight years old, Josey was expected to saddle her horse and herd cattle. "There was a job to be done, and feelings didn't matter." Indoors, Josey's mother and grandmother expected her to be quiet and "behave," meaning, "act like an adult." Having to push down fear, discomfort, surprise, resentment, and other negative emotions caused Josey to disconnect from her feelings.

A life-long lockdown of her emotions eventually manifested as fibromyalgia, with Josey's muscles locked up tight and in pain. During our first sessions, when asked how past or present situations made her feel, she would say, "Not good." That was as close to naming a feeling as she could get. Feeling numb to pain meant she didn't feel any joy in her life, either.

---

*Note: Client names from session examples included in this book have been changed to protect the privacy of the people involved.

DEVELOPING EMOTIONAL RESILIENCE:

As a child, my older brother and I had a 42-inch-tall inflatable punching toy. Due to a weighted bottom, no matter how many times we tried to knock this clown down, he would bounce right back. This is resilience.

A child who can experience adversity, and then identify and process uncomfortable feelings, learns emotional resilience, or, the ability to "bounce back" from distressing situations. Conversely, telling a child to "toughen up" undermines emotional resilience.

We need to allow our child to feel *all* of the feelings that may arise throughout the day.

Studies show stronger mental and physical health is associated with experiencing a range of emotions, instead of experiencing pressure to be happy or content all of the time. This means allowing our child to feel sad, bored, or frustrated, and then helping them to see those feelings as useful feedback.

The ability to notice emotional reactions is a valuable gift. Negative emotions are signals that we are out of sync with life. Whether feeling stressed, angry, or sad, upsetting emotions may motivate our child to change behavior or recognize unsafe individuals and situations. Positive emotions can help our child to recognize preferences for experiences worth repeating, and to identify trustworthy individuals.

Part of emotional resilience is coming to accept the ups and downs of emotions in response to the world around us. Like the peaks and valleys of a heart monitor confirming you are alive, part of life is feeling emotional highs and lows.

Validating emotional or physical pain allows our child to bounce back from hurts, instead of break.

As parents, we can't protect our child from every hurt. However, routinely and repeatedly validating our child when he or she feels sad, angry, guilty, afraid, disappointed, or stressed develops our child's capacity to reframe and rebound from life's hard knocks.

Chapter 3: Feelings Matter

"It's not what happens to us, but our response
to what happens to us that hurts us."
– Stephen Covey

While babysitting for a friend, her two young children asked to watch the Disney movie, *Monsters, Inc.* In the film, the monsters believe they must scare children to generate power for their city, until a human girl follows the monsters back into their world.

Nestled on either side of my husband, with a big bowl of popcorn, the boys were ready to enjoy the show. Little Owen, just two-and-a-half, surprised my husband by naming emotions he felt while watching the movie. He would whisper, "Scary, scary . . ." under his breath in certain parts, and my husband would reassure him that everything was going to be okay. Owen said, ". . . sad . . ." at another place in the movie, and my husband told him: "But they are going to be happy in a minute," which consoled Owen.

Interestingly, the first time a six-legged, purple villain named "Randall" appeared on the screen, Owen whispered, "Creepy . . ." Even at his young age, he could sense and express bad and good impressions and feelings.

Children are clearly aware of the emotions around them. Research sponsored by the *Zero to Three Organization* found that as early as three to five months old, children can feel sad or fearful. At three months, a child can begin to "sense and be affected by a parent's mood, such as angry or sad" (Lerner, 2017).

Researchers have identified that humans are born with a small number of built-in feelings, along with corresponding facial and body expressions. These basic emotions are:

- Happiness
- Sadness
- Anger
- Fear
- Surprise
- Shame
- Disgust

Each fundamental feeling is designed to be activated by a variety of stimuli. For example, infants will smile in response to a happy face, or a familiar soothing voice. Conversely, most infants naturally cry when they're hungry, feel pain, or are startled by a loud sound.

Children innately feel and release emotions that arise *until* they are taught to suppress their natural emotional responses.

A child is taught to disregard feelings when told things like, "Quit crying, you're not a baby," or, "Big boys aren't afraid of the dark," or, "Don't be such a drama queen." Comments like these undermine a child's confidence to trust that what he or she is feeling matters.

In the previous example, my husband validated Owen's emotional reactions during the movie to help Owen feel safe. It would be cruel for my husband to have said, "Don't be such a wimp!" or, "There is nothing to be afraid of, it's just a movie." Yet, in everyday interactions with our children, we often downplay their feelings.

For example, our child might come home from school reporting that a classmate laughed at her drawing. Instead of asking how it made him or her feel, we often give advice such as, "Don't worry what other people think," or, "Not everyone is good at the same things. You're better at soccer."

Though meaning well with our counsel, we often erode our child's confidence that his or her feelings matter.

Feelings matter.

In fact, feelings *are* matter. In the past, you may not have consciously been aware of these vibrations, but you have certainly sensed them. Have you ever walked into a room where two people have been fighting, and feel the tension in the air without hearing a word? Have you found yourself spontaneously breaking into laughter after hearing a baby's laugh? Are there people whose actual presence just suck the life out of you--or conversely--energize and elevate your mood? In each case, you are tuning into the "vibe," or "vibrational energy," of emotions around you.

Scientific evidence exhibits that emotion is literally "energy in motion" (E=motion). Dr. Masaru Emoto made waves with his research demonstrating the effect of thoughts, words, and feelings on water molecules. His book, *The Hidden Messages in Water,* features photos of frozen water crystals which dramatically changed structure after water bottles were simply labeled with words that expressed different emotions. Spring water exposed to loving, positive words created complex snowflake patterns. In contrast, water exposed to negative messages formed dull, asymmetrical patterns (Emoto, 2010).

The images below show water taken from jars labeled with different phrases:

Water charged with words,
"You disgust me"

Water charged with words,
"Thank You"

Clearly, words and emotions can affect a measurable change in the physical world. Since the human body content is more than 70% water, it makes sense that thoughts and feelings can literally affect how our body responds to stress or adversity.

Feelings are simply an emotional reaction to what we experience.

Some emotions stimulate your heart to race, your stomach to churn, or your adrenalin to rush. Other emotions allow your body to relax, your mood to lift, and your mind to calm.

The bottom line is that we all want to feel good, and our kids want to feel good, too. When any of us feel bad, the automatic response is to want to avoid the situations, the people, or the thoughts that are creating those negative feelings. This fear of feeling our feelings was perfectly illustrated in a dialogue from *The Lego Batman Movie*.

Alfred asks Batman: Do you want to talk about how you're feeling?

Batman replies: What? No! I don't want to do that! No, no, no, no, no! I don't talk about feelings, Alfred. I don't have any; I've never seen one. I'm a night-stalking, crime-fighting vigilante, and a heavy-metal rapping machine. I don't feel anything emotionally, except for rage, 24/7, 365, at a million percent, and if you think that there's something behind that, then you're crazy. Good night, Alfred.

Alfred: Sir, it's morning.

Why feelings matter

Feelings combine with thoughts
which lead to beliefs and behaviors.

Think of a time when you received bad news, witnessed an accident, or watched video footage of a national disaster on TV. When we experience highly surprising, disturbing, or consequential events, our brain creates a "flashbulb" moment, vividly capturing the memory. Linked with strong emotions, these memories are highly resistant to  being forgotten. Left un-validated, these "freeze-frame" moments can turn into pain points. Even so, studies suggest these "snapshots" do not always represent accurate pictures of events (Mastin, 2018).

When a child experiences trauma, the situation may generate a broken belief, such as, *"Because this happened, I'm never going to be _____"* *(loved, included, successful)*, or a limiting label, such as, *"I am _____"* *(powerless, unlovable, a failure).* Based on what happened, our child comes to conclusions about his or her worth *and* place in the world.

Webster defines **belief** as "a *feeling* of being sure something is true" (emphasis added). So, a belief is nothing more than strong emotion attached to a thought. The frightening part is that our belief doesn't have to be accurate; we just need to *think* we are right.

Beliefs color how we look at the world, just as if we were wearing colored glasses.

Beliefs influence our child's behavior. Once something is believed to be true, the brain seeks evidence to support that belief. The more proof the mind finds, the more deeply entrenched the belief becomes. Like car tires carving ruts into a dirt road, eventually, the wheels can't get out of the grooves.

Beliefs become self-fulfilling prophecies.

Feelings of shame may lead someone to believe they are not enough, or that they are a failure. Once a child decides they are dumb, they may stop studying for tests or turning in homework. If a child believes that no one likes them, they may struggle to make friends because they don't make eye contact, smile, or speak up.

Unhealthy beliefs may cause a lack of motivation, as well as a surge in avoidance, helplessness, or depression. Then, the behavior reinforces the belief, and it's a vicious cycle.

From the time Michael was seven, he believed he was a failure. He struggled in school with dyslexia and ADHD. His mom met with teachers, and together they created accommodations for his learning disabilities, but he said those things just reinforced to him that they didn't believe he could succeed. Once Michael adopted the belief that he was a failure, he continued to underachieve in school, graduating with a 1.8 G.P.A. He struggled to keep a job, his marriage ended in divorce, and he turned to addictive substances and behaviors to cope. He said it wasn't worth trying because he knew he would fail anyway. Finally, at age 35, we were able to validate the pain, allowing him to claim a better belief: "I am successful when I try."

Stored in the subconscious mind, beliefs are like programming a GPS with coordinates that dictate where the driver will go. Each turn is directed, and should the driver attempt to travel another way, the GPS will recalculate and continue sending instructions and reminders to reach the original destination.

The subconscious mind's will is stronger than the conscious mind's wants.

Once in place, these hidden procedures become the dominant driver of behavior. For example, when a child believes, "nobody likes me," no amount of love, attention, or persuasion will change that programming. Unless and until the situation which generated distressing emotions and limiting beliefs is validated, nothing will change, and healing can't happen.

Unresolved feelings may generate broken beliefs:

- I am not safe
- I am not enough

- I am a failure
- I can't trust anyone
- Something's wrong with me
- I am always on guard
- I can't stand up for myself
- I don't know how to be happy/feel joy
- I can't keep up (e.g.: I can't meet expectations-- whether in athletics, school, family, work, etc.)
- I am unwanted
- I can't control my body
- I deserve to be punished
- I hate my body
- Feelings are dangerous
- I am alone
- I am empty inside
- I am powerless
- I am unlovable
- Change is dangerous
- Everything is a mess
- I don't belong
- I am overwhelmed/lost/trapped
- I don't love or trust myself
- No one cares about/understands me
- I expect more from myself than others
- I can't let go of my addiction
- Nothing I do works
- There is no way out
- I am not important to God

Limiting beliefs can also be easily identified when our child makes broad generalizations with terms like: "always," "never," "everyone," and "no one":

- I *always* get the blame
- I *never* get to do anything fun
- *Everyone* is mad at me
- *No one* likes me

Broken beliefs can lead to harmful behaviors.

*Ashley was feeling anxious and overwhelmed. With finals looming, she felt stressed and tired from not sleeping. Math was her hardest subject, and she constantly compared her grades to others', reporting, "**Everybody** is doing good, but me." Feeling friendless, alone, and afraid, Ashley began to isolate herself. After receiving a poor grade on midterms, Ashley had dug her fingernails into her palms until she drew blood. For a few minutes, her feelings of hopelessness subsided.*

Soon, self-injury became a ritual. Anytime Ashley felt overwhelmed, she would "release" the bad feelings by scratching her arm as hard as she could with her fingernails, or by cutting her arm with a razor blade. Carefully hiding the marks to avoid questions, the relief she felt was only temporary, and contributed to more broken beliefs about her worth. Ashley told me, "Sometimes we don't find ways to heal, we just find ways to deal . . ." Once Ashley learned how to recognize and release negative thoughts and feelings with Emotional 911, she was able to choose self-care over self-harm options.

Seeking to relieve stress, children and teens can turn to unhealthy coping strategies such as:

- soothing (food/sex)
- numbing (alcohol/drugs)
- distracting (video games/social media/shopping)
- self-harming (cutting/picking/hair-pulling/head-banging)

Each action provides only *temporary relief* from tension and other bad feelings without resolving them. An additional danger comes as these behaviors develop into compelling habits, or lifelong addictions.

Emotional Danger Zones

Generation Vexed

Today's children and teens live with constant comparing and the concern of being judged. Young people are being "sifted, sorted and ranked" by teachers, employers and peers (Curran, 2018). This push for perfectionism triggers psychological turmoil and harsh self-criticism. Plus, teens are flooded with anticipatory fears, such as failure, uncertainty, change or rejection, privately struggling with feelings of self-doubt.

A main factor contributing to increased stress, perfectionism, depression and anxiety in teens comes from constant access to cell phones and social media. San Diego State University professor, Jean Twenge, refers to teens born after 1995 as iGen--the Smartphone-obsessed generation.

Twenge suggests a correlation between mental health issues and cell phone usage by children, stating, "It's probably not a coincidence that mental health issues began to increase around 2012, the first year that the percentage of Americans with a Smartphone rose above 50 percent.

Spending a lot of time on a Smartphone is correlated with unhappiness. For example, eighth graders who spend two or more hours a day on social media are 56 percent more likely to be unhappy than those who spend less time on their phones. Other studies suggest that social media leads to unhappiness, rather than unhappiness leading to social media use" (Twenge, 2017).

According to Pew Research Center, 95% of teens have a Smartphone, spending on average *nine hours per day* submerged in virtual screen stimulation. Snapchat, Pinterest, and Twitter all shape a teen's social sense of self-worth.

We are conditioned by media exposure to believe life has to look a certain way for us to be happy. Many children (and adults) compare their ordinary lives to Facebook stories of big moments, special events and social belonging.

Social media platforms like Instagram can impact body image and identities, causing a compare/despair cycle as teens are faced with constant comparisons in the palms of their hands. Moreover, young women measure themselves against, "unrealistic, largely curated, filtered and Photoshopped versions of reality" (Fox, 2017). Suffering from

"Snapchat dysmorphia," many young women believe they are not pretty unless there is a filter on their face. They Google, "What's wrong with me?" and question whether they are enough.

Additionally, as parents we need to watch the messages we send to our daughters about appearance vs. ability. Continually praising, "You look so pretty," may create a belief that physical beauty matters more for girls than other dimensions—like academics, arts, or sports—and can equate self-esteem based on perceived physical attractiveness.

Beyond negative body image, social media affects user sleep patterns, and generates a sense of "FOMO" – fear of missing out – as teens scroll through pictures, tracking the social activities of peers. Teens say that even when they are not looking at their phone, they are constantly thinking about it. The craving for "likes" becomes a chemical addiction as powerful as gambling or drug use. 63% of Instagram users say that using this app makes them feel miserable, yet they are unable to break free.

Cyberbullying has increased with nearly 60 percent of teens saying they've been harassed online. A 2018 PEW survey shows increases in offensive name-calling, receiving unwanted explicit images, physical threats and the spreading of false  rumors. No longer are hurtful words just spoken at school. Sadly, now a child can bring the bully home in his or her pocket. Whether in your face or on your Facebook page, bullying is wounding.

Wise parents will consider limiting screen time for children and teens, and no child should have access to a Smartphone after bedtime. Twenge advises up to one hour of screen time per day is tolerated. However, youths spending 3-5 hours per day on devices show a 30% increase in suicide ideation. More than 5 hours per day pushes that risk to 71%.

Crusader, Collin Kartchner, is on a mission to teach parents how social media is stealing kids' joy. His #savethekids movement likens giving a child a Smartphone to handing them a gun, noting spiking teen suicide rates (https://savethekids.us).

If you are seeing symptoms of social media anxiety and depression, encourage your child to do a temporary screen fast. Lead by example and disconnect to reconnect. Most teens find a happiness boost within days of taking a social media break (Heid, 2017).

There is also growing concern over teens, especially boys,

 who may be spending too much time submerged and isolated playing video games. Gaming addiction is now being considered for inclusion in the Diagnostic and Statistical Manual of Mental Disorders (Conrad).

When played in moderation, video games are a simple form of entertainment. However, when gaming becomes an obsession, escape, or avoidance tactic, a host of negative consequences result, including:

- neglect (of personal hygiene, physical activity, sleep, nutrition and other responsibilities)
- financial (spending money on expensive upgrades; missing work to game)
- family arguments (over time limits, neglect, and other issues)
- academic (ignoring study time and/or homework deadlines and other similar responsibilities)
- interpersonal (minimized face-to-face interaction and/or a disconnection from the world)
- psychological (with depression, low-self-esteem, high stress, and/or social anxiety)

When our child is hurting, we need to know how to help him or her feel better right now.

It is our beliefs that determine how we interpret what happens in life. Often a child can't see beyond their own pain or alternatives to their actions. Teaching a child emotional hygiene is key. Just as daily routines of cleanliness contribute to a healthy  body, daily habits of emotional detox support well-being in the mind.

For example: When a child uses the word "stress" to describe any aspect of life, we can remind him or her that pressure, worry or tension is often self-generated. It can come from trying to control things that are not within our control. It can be triggered by unrealistic expectations or being too attached to certain outcomes.

Instead, help a child recognize what is within his or her control. Our response is our responsibility. Broken beliefs can be mended or replaced. Peace is possible, even in the midst of challenges.

Employing emotional first aid can bring immediate relief. Just like programming in a new set of coordinates on a GPS, proper validation allows our child's subconscious brain to shift, exchanging broken beliefs and behaviors for something better.

The most important beliefs a child can hold are:

- ♥ *I am safe*
- ♥ *I am worthy*
- ♥ *I am loved*

As we foster these essential perceptions of identity, we map a route to emotional resilience and healing for our child.

Chapter 4: The Value of Validation

"Courage isn't inside; it's external.
It comes from someone else
telling you they believe in you."
- Simon Sinek

Have you ever wondered why a kiss often works as well as a bandage in consoling a hurt child? Perhaps the reason a kiss can comfort is the value of validation it gives.

Webster defines validation as, *"confirming the truthfulness of something or to make somebody feel valued, and that his or her thoughts are worthwhile."*

While seeming counterintuitive, validating a child's difficulty, no matter how big or small, may prevent the issue from increasing. As parents, we must be ready to supply not only physical but emotional life-saving care via validation - the foundation of emotional first aid.

Validation acknowledges:

- **something painful happened**

- **the hurt is greater than you can bear alone, and**

- **someone believes you are going to be okay.**

57

Let's look more closely at why validation is not just nice or needed, but absolutely necessary.

Something painful happened.

Getting through life without experiencing painful events and emotional upheavals is impossible. Most days are filled with happy and sad moments, which pass quickly like wind blowing through trees. The branches might bend and sway, but will bounce back to their original shape once the wind stops. On rare occasions, a strong wind or a heavy snowfall can cause a branch to snap.

Likewise, we don't know which incident may become a breaking or "pain point," for our child. It might be a bad grade on a test, an unkind word from a peer, or not making the team.

Anything can be perceived as trauma by the brain.

Almost every family has a story about forgetting a child somewhere; a friend's house, a gas station, or even *Home Alone* - as featured in a trilogy of hit movies with that title. Most families tell the story jokingly, and it's considered "no harm, no foul."

With my daughter, Katie, I was baffled at how my tardiness in picking her up from school could turn this formerly-happy ten-year-old into a clingy, insecure ball of fear . . . until she reminded me that she had been forgotten five years before.

We "forgot" our daughter at a neighborhood park. That's not completely accurate; it was more like a series of misunderstandings.

After our son's baseball game at a local park, then-five-year-old Katie wanted to stay and play with her girlfriends who were twins. Hungry and tired, we were anxious to get home in time for our favorite TV show, which we had neglected to program for recording (back in the days before DVR).

While I was making plans with the twins' mom, my husband and son had already started walking across the park. Katie suddenly changed her mind about staying to play, so she and I headed toward our truck. Katie was riding a scooter on the sidewalk, and I cut across the grass, through the parking lot, and across the street to where the truck was parked.

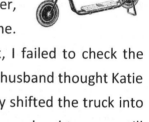

Since Katie was riding a scooter, I assumed she had arrived before me. Hopping in the front seat of the truck, I failed to check the back seat to be sure she was there. My husband thought Katie was staying to play, and he immediately shifted the truck into gear and drove away. Unfortunately, our daughter was still waiting to cross the street, and watched us drive away without her.

Arriving home, we hurried into the house. The guys turned on the TV while I started dinner, all without noticing Katie was missing. Being a smart and resourceful child, Katie wisely returned to the twins' mother and told her we had left without her.

When our home phone rang, I was shocked as the twins' mother explained what had happened, and how Katie was still with her, at the park. I quickly returned to the park, which was fewer than five minutes from our house. Katie had obviously been crying, but once I arrived and hugged her, she seemed fine. We went home, ate dinner, and watched our show. I had no idea that this seemingly-minor incident would create a "pain point" waiting to be triggered five years later when I was late picking Katie up from school.

This story is difficult for me to share, because it's so easy to feel ashamed that a TV show was more important to me than my daughter's safety and well-being. I felt guilty that *I had caused* this traumatic event in her life. Is that true? Not necessarily. As a small child, my brother-in-law was accidentally left behind at a gas station. Although it took his family hours to notice and return, he tells the story while laughing about the experience.

The truth is that we can't know which life experience is going to become a pain point.

Two people can witness or experience the same event and have completely different reactions. What would be a fleeting incident for one person can become a life-altering event for another. Problems tend to arise when a painful experience is not properly validated, mending the incident in the mind.

In the end, it's not the situation or what has happened that creates a trauma or pain point, but the feelings and meaning attached by the brain about what happened.

The hurt is greater than you can bear alone.

From the moment of birth, children let us know when they experience discomfort, pain, or distress. It would be unthinkable to ignore a baby's cry for help without checking for possible causes, or trying to comfort.

Yet, as children age, it's not uncommon for well-meaning parents to minimize a child's pain, worry, or difficulty for fear of making them wimpy or whiny. There is clearly a place for not overreacting to every little bump and bruise, however, showing empathy gives a child the comforting reassurance of being heard, understood, and validated.

For example, when a child falls down, scrapes a knee and begins to cry, instead of saying, "You're all right," or, "Don't cry," we can acknowledge the pain with a short, simple phrase such as, "Ouch! That must have hurt!" As we genuinely mirror a child's pain with our voice and with our body language, this validation allows him or her to determine whether or not he or she is okay, and go back to playing. If not, the child will feel safe asking for additional help.

In fifth grade, I was playing at a friend's house and injured my wrist. I went home crying, and my mom, who always told me I had "a low pain threshold," suggested I soak my wrist in cold water at the bathroom sink. Hours later, when the pain didn't diminish, my mom decided to take me to the emergency room. Upon examination, my wrist was, in fact, broken. I remember feeling sad and betrayed that my mom didn't initially believe me when I said I was really hurt, and that she didn't seek to comfort me. In that moment, all I needed was for her to say she was sorry I had been injured, and ask how she could help me feel better.

Acknowledging painful feelings doesn't stunt emotional growth; it actually enhances emotional resilience. Validating an "owie" with a kiss and/or kindness tells our child we recognize the shock, surprise, or difficulty of what happened, as much as the physical wound itself.

It may be even more important to acknowledge hurts you can't see on the outside.

How do we know when a child needs emotional support? We can become attuned to the emotional signals being broadcast. Before the digital age, when you wanted to find a radio station, you had to manually adjust the dial until the signal was the strongest. This required effort to remove the static and hone in on the frequency.

As parents, we may need to adjust, and perhaps "fine-

tune" our ability to receive the emotional distress signals emitted by our child. There may be physical cues through body language: slumped shoulders, eyes downcast and/or crossed arms, as if the body is curling up into a ball to protect itself. Or, we might notice some of the following emotional distress signals.

Common Emotional Distress Signals:

- Acting irritable or moody
- Withdrawing from activities that used to be enjoyed
- Complaining more than usual about school or friends
- Displaying fearful reactions (such as clinging to a parent or avoiding certain people)
- Sleeping or eating too much or too little
- Routinely expressing worries
- Unusual social media postings that may seem like a cry for help
- Expressing anger or annoyance at little things
- Feeling "sick," such as frequent complaints of stomachaches or headaches (when doctors find no cause). Be sure to take notice if these symptoms increase in certain situations, (such as before a test, a sports game, or leaving home) or after spending time with specific individuals.
- Negative self-talk or criticism of the world around them ("I'm dumb," or, "Nothing is fun")

As a parent, we empathize by using our ears and eyes. Don't just listen for verbal cues of discomfort. Watch for what a child may not say. Should we recognize emotional distress signals and offer support, our child might push us away saying nothing is wrong, or that he or she is fine. **Trust your instincts and follow up.**

Go to your child, and simply sit next to him or her as a show of support. Often, we don't need to say anything. Other times, our child might need a little coaxing, such as driving to get a soda, or to rent a movie.

Scientific evidence suggests boys and men call for *side-by-side conversations* instead of *face-to-face confrontation* to feel safe to communicate. So, sit next to your son at the counter, table or in the car when you need to converse about concerns.

Prioritize being present and being available, especially at the crossroads - when children are going to and coming from school, sports, play dates, work, or other activities. Never knowing when distress may strike, we want to be available to acknowledge hurts as they happen.

Someone believes you are going to be okay.

As parents, our reassurance reminds our child of his or her own resilience. When we validate our child's feelings, we create and reinforce secure attachments. Adding physical touch enhances validation, as hugging imprints a child on a cellular level to promote bonding (Satir, 2014).

In 1958, researcher John Bowlby first coined the term, "Attachment Theory," which suggests that a strong emotional and physical attachment to at least one primary caregiver is critical to personal development. According to Bowlby, children have a universal need to seek close proximity with their caregiver when under stress or when threatened (Bowlby, 1969).

Around the same time, Henry Harlow was studying how newborn Rhesus monkeys bonded with substitute, artificial mothers. His attachment experiments demonstrated that infant monkeys preferred a soft, terry cloth "mother" over a wire one, even though milk was only dispensed from the wire-frame surrogate. His explanation of their action? Attachment develops from a mother providing "tactile comfort," which suggests a biological need to touch and cling to something - or better yet, *someone* - for emotional comfort when distressed (Prior, 2006).

Healthy attachment gives our child confidence that he or she can turn to us for help and healing.

The **single most important factor** influencing resilience and recovery is providing a child with our consistent and supportive presence. Secure attachment is not about being a perfect parent, but about maintaining empathetic communication to help our child recover from inevitable upsets that occur.

Just as comforting a child who receives a vaccination can reduce the pain of this stressful event, a strong, nurturing relationship with our child helps reduce the body's response to troubling events. Once that bond is in place, parents don't even have to be present to lessen the impact of stressful situations. Simply being able to talk to a parent after an upsetting incident allows a child's stress level to quickly return to normal (Graham, 2018).

Advocating neither "helicopter" nor "snowplow" parenting styles (with parents who hover over or clear the path for their child), nor a hands-off, "let-them-bleed" style of parenting, the goal is provide a happy middle ground of fostering physical fortitude and emotional resilience.

Validation is *NOT* rescuing, enabling, weakening, coddling, or babying. In actuality, validation is empowering. In effect, validation says, "No matter what has happened to you, I believe you are going to be okay. You are going to overcome, survive, and thrive by turning this stumbling block into a stepping stone."

**Our validation offers the connection
and life-saving encouragement
necessary to overcome and heal.**

We never know when our aid will be required. Assurance that we will listen without judgment, empathize with compassion, and encourage via validation can generate the emotional resilience and healing we seek for our child.

*Validation is love in action.
Like the song says,
"What the world needs now is
love, sweet love; no, not just for
some, but for everyone."*

Song by Jackie DeShannon

Chapter 5: Making a Hero –
The Validation Recipe

"We do not have to become heroes overnight.
Just a step at a time, meeting each thing that comes up . . .
discovering we have the strength to stare it down."
- Eleanor Roosevelt

Imagine a first responder arriving on a scene to help a victim whose heart has stopped beating. Supplied with a defibrillator machine (used to jump start the heart), the emergency medical technician (EMT) desires to remedy the situation. Regrettably, untrained in the correct steps required to apply this life-saving measure, he can't provide aid.

Likewise, in times of emergency, we can't provide our child with life-saving validation unless we know the proper sequence.

How to Validate:

Have you ever made homemade ice cream? My sister-in-law, Molly, and her family, host an annual July fireworks-and-ice-cream party. She and her mother prepare for weeks in advance, whipping up their own 31 flavors with yummy delights like, "Oatmeal Cookie Dough," "Raspberry Ripple," and "Salted Caramel." When asked how they came up with so many creations, I was surprised to learn that many of the flavors began with the same basic recipe before Molly added other ingredients.

Similarly, the steps of validation are like a basic recipe. On occasion you will need to insert additional ingredients, customizing for specific needs. We will cover those in future chapters. However, the original formula will satisfy in most situations.

Validation Basic Recipe

Our Validation Basic Recipe doesn't involve making ice cream. Instead, we are building a Hero Sandwich with a hearty bun on the outside, and three essential ingredients stacked in the middle.

Validation Hero Sandwich

The "bun" is our genuine compassion and caring. It begins with the phrase, "I'm sorry," and ends with the question, "Will you be okay?" This concern and  connection hold the rest of the nourishing ingredients securely in place.

The "meat" of validation employs **three key questions** we ask our child concerning what has happened or is happening, to guide them to the other side of hurting.

A hero is a person who is admired for courage, bravery, or achievement. We want our child to develop courage in facing uncomfortable and painful events, trusting that they can

W-I-N, or overcome challenges, using the central ingredients of the sandwich.

As we practice this "winning" recipe, our child will eventually be able to build his or her own Hero Sandwich with a similar sequence.

This basic recipe works for any age (including adults), because it covers the three tenets of validation: something painful happened to you, the hurt is greater than you can bear alone, and someone believes you are going to be okay.

Obviously, not every hurt requires all five steps. Yet, the first step of expressing empathy using the phrase, "I'm sorry . . ." is always appropriate.

Sometimes a child may fear speaking up. Should we recognize an emotional distress signal, we want to invite our child to tell the story of what is causing their pain. Initiating the Validation Hero Recipe allows us to invite conversation and assess the level of Emotional 911 required.

Validation permits a child to W-I-N, transforming troubles into triumphs.

As we learn and apply the Validation Basic Recipe, we show a child that we understand not only the *situation*, but how he or she *feels* as a result.

Let's apply the Validation Hero Recipe in a simple example:

After dinner one night, five-year-old Jonathan told his parents that a classmate was mean to him on the playground at school, reporting, "He hurt my 'feel-bads.'"

Top Bun:

"I'm sorry that happened to you."

When our child hurts, we hurt. Making it easy to jump into Mama-or-Papa-Bear mode, we may find ourselves railing against the perpetrator or situation that caused our child to feel bad. There is a time and a place for that, but the pressing priority necessitates acknowledgement of our child's "feel-bads."

If you saw your child being crushed by a rock, your goal would not be to find out who put the rock there, or to get under the rock and feel what your child is feeling. Your only priority would be to remove the rock.

Simply sitting with our child, holding a hand, giving a hug or a pat on the back while sincerely speaking the words, "I'm sorry you were hurt," can often lift the weight of the rock. Sometimes, that is all that is needed for our child to feel better.

Attachment researchers, Simpson and Rholes, identified that, "lack of an emotionally-supportive response by a loved one at the moment of trauma can demolish the security of a relationship" (Simpson, 1998). Like an eclipse blocking out hundreds of smaller positive events, lack of validation may undermine a child's confidence that we care about his or her pain, and will be there when we're needed most. This is a pass or fail test.

Genuine empathy is an invitation to connect, encouraging our child to examine and express feelings. Often, this acknowledgement--recognizing something hurtful has happened--is enough to allow a child to let go of the incident and any accompanying painful feelings.

Modeling compassion, telling a child we are sorry he or she experienced a physical hurt or emotional scrape, supplies immediate relief. This practice develops deepening trust that we will be there for small and big issues.

**For a list of questions
that encourage conversation,
see Chapter 6.**

When Jonathan told his parents that his feelings had been hurt that day at school, Dad turned off the TV, Mom gave him a hug, and said, "I'm sorry that happened. Can you tell us more?"

Notice how Jonathan's parents showed a desire to comfort their son using two essential elements necessary for validation: physical touch and empathetic listening.

**Now, load the Validation Hero Sandwich
with the *three key ingredients* to help your child
W-I-N in the face of difficulty.**

Ask, "What's the <u>worst</u> part?"

When our child is upset, sometimes it's easy to get lost in the story of what happened without knowing *which part caused the pain*. This question helps our child target how the injury is impacting him or her. Providing an opportunity for a child to put the hurt being felt into words helps us, as parents, know what is causing the pain, but it also helps our child better know himself or herself.

Telling the story short-circuits the incident's power to continue to harm a child, or cause them pain. Creating space for self-reflection allows our child to develop the ability to evaluate inner conflicts, reactions, and needs.

Imagine the story of what happened like a round target, with circles getting smaller and smaller until you reach the bull's-eye. By focusing on the center, we can get to the heart of the matter: the fears and feelings.

When physically hurt, our child may be worried he or she can't participate in an upcoming activity. When emotionally injured, this question spotlights the meaning our child is assigning to the event - often feelings of worth or safety.

Dr. Christiane Northrup tells of a time when her seven-year-old daughter had cut herself on a blade of grass. Calmly holding her daughter's finger under some cold water, Christiane saw it was only a tiny cut. Her daughter looked up and uttered what Christiane considered a major healing principle: **"It didn't hurt until I got scared."**

- (Northrup, *Women's Bodies, Women's Wisdom*, 2006)

Jonathan told his parents a classmate said he was too slow to be included in a game of Tag with the other boys. After listening to the details of Jonathon's story, his dad asked, "What's the worst part?" Jonathan replied, "I'm afraid they won't let me play any of the games, and I'll have to be alone at recess."

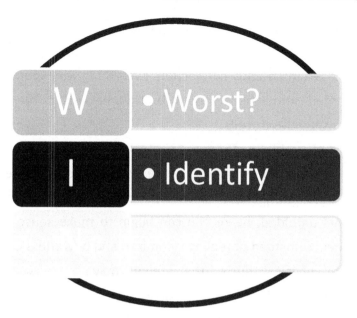

Identify: Ask, "How do you feel?"

In Pixar's hit movie, *Inside Out*, the emotions live in a headquarters inside eleven-year-old Riley's brain. Every incident she experiences is encapsulated in a "memory ball," colored by the predominant emotion. When a memory is happy, the orb is yellow for joy; it's blue for sadness, red for anger, green for disgust, and purple for fear.

**It's not what happened that causes lasting harm,
it is how one *feels* about it that colors the memory.**

This movie offered a fantastic representation of what is happening in the body in response to the world around us. There *is* a mind-body connection. Everything we experience is recorded somewhere in our body, whether in the brain, organs, tissues or cells.

When a child experiences a shock or a trauma, he or she often doesn't know how to process the incident. As we help our child safely examine *what* happened, and perhaps *how* events unfolded, he or she can begin to make sense of the sequence, instead of feeling victimized and powerless.

For physical hurts, the feeling may simply be "hurt," or, "scared." For emotional slights, there are infinite shades and variations of feelings that may arise. We will discuss how to develop a child's ability to better notice and name feelings in Chapter 14: Name and Tame.

This can be especially important if someone hurts our child, or makes them feel afraid or uncomfortable. Sometimes, children are reluctant to report an uncomfortable event or situation, fearing they might get in trouble, or get someone else in trouble. Whether physically or emotionally wounded by a family member, church leader, school teacher, friend or neighbor, our child needs to feel safe telling us if they are hurting.

Shame teaches a child to hide what happened.
When you hide, you can't get help.

Through repeated moments of validation, our child will come to want to unload his or her experiences and upsetting emotions to find relief. Often, a child is unaware of the connection between what has happened or is happening, and the distress signals being sent.

With younger children, they may need our help to make the connection between their actions and feelings. We can say, "I see you are kicking the chair . . . are you feeling frustrated that we have to clean up now?" As we help our child make the association between upsetting feelings and his or her reactions, we teach a child to recognize what is needed in that moment, and to feel safe to ask for support.

Our goal as a listener is not to repair or resolve, debate or defend what happened, but to allow our child to feel seen, heard, and understood. Validation means letting our child know we can see the situation from his or her perspective.

Whether or not we agree with a child's perception, we can still validate whatever is felt. Research confirms that having someone show us support is the single best predictor of human resilience.

Jonathan's secure attachment and trust that his parents would validate his emotions allowed him to share his pain. When Jonathan's parents asked him, "How does it make you feel to be alone on the playground at recess?" Jonathan replied that he felt mad, sad, and lonely. Acknowledging his feelings as appropriate and understandable, Jonathan's mom said, "I would be sad, too, if that happened to me."

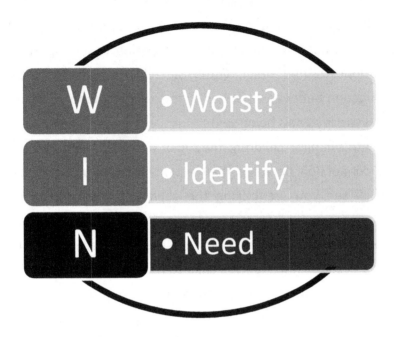

Ask, "What do you <u>need</u> to make things better?"

The goal is to help our child identify what is needed in the moment to feel better. Does he or she need to cry, moan, or yell? Scribble or write on a page? Does he or she need to run around the block or punch a pillow?

Some parents give food as a soother, such as offering a cookie or other treat. This practice may lead to masking or stuffing feelings in the future, and is not favored.

Many children get in the habit of looking to us as a "Google Parent," expecting us to provide all of the answers. This is the time when *we* want to ask the questions, not solve the problem for our child.

Often a child's first response to the question, "What can make it better?" is, "I don't know," or, "Nothing!" As a parent, we want to make things better right away, and might notice the urge to tell our child what we think *should* happen to make things better.

"Should-ing" is shaming.

Instead, empowering our child to select a solution on his or her own encourages self-awareness, self-soothing, and self-assurance.

One of the best ways to show support without solving the problem is through physical touch. Physical connection, whether with hugs or hand-holding, stimulates a host of healing responses in the body (Fahad, 2015). These include:

- releasing oxytocin (a trust hormone) and serotonin (a happiness hormone) in the brain
- stimulating the release of endorphins which block pain pathways
- balancing the nervous system
- decreasing the heart rate, and
- allowing for the exchange of feelings

If a child remains stuck deciding what will make things better, we can ask permission before we give our opinion, input, or suggestions.

Offering, "Would you like my help to make a list of ideas that might help you feel better?" can grease the wheels and get ideas flowing. Suggesting *temporary* diversions can also relieve the pressure a child feels to find an immediate solution.

Successful and resilient people are problem solvers, looking not just for one, but multiple solutions to a problem. This is a skill worth modeling and teaching. However, it may be a good idea to save our best suggestions for last, since the first few may often get shot down by a child or a teen.

Physical actions can help the body's emotional system "digest" or process feelings quickly and efficiently. When we show our child it is safe to be present with what is being felt instead of running away, the body has the ability to heal itself emotionally and physically.

Did you know . . . ?

After escaping an attack, deer will shake, ducks will flap their wings, and rabbits will vibrate. These tremors are how the central nervous system in mammals discharges excess tension and adrenalin to calm the body down. The human body has the same capacity through rapid muscle contraction and relaxation, sometimes felt as butterflies in the stomach, knocking knees, or the body "shaking like a leaf."

While these responses are often seen as a sign of weakness, tremors can turn down the central nervous system's automatic fight-flight-or-freeze response, releasing built-up energy and tension.

So, give a child permission to "shake away" any stressful feelings that might surface.

http://treaustralia.com.au/tre-info/neurogenic-tremors/

Consider using humor, imagination, and creativity to short circuit the "helpless-hurting" feedback loop. Propose something outrageous, like pretending to swim through peanut butter, shaking the body like a wet dog, or acting out an injury in rewind mode.

When Jonathon was asked what he needed to feel better, he eventually decided that if he was excluded from one group, he would look for another classmate who was alone and invite him to play. Had this solution been suggested to him, he most likely would have found a reason to reject it. As his own idea, he will find a way to make it work.

Bottom Bun:

Will you be okay?

Ask: "Will you be okay?"

When our child is hurting, we would do anything to help him or her feel better immediately. However, this doesn't mean it's our job to make everything okay. We cannot right every wrong, or smooth every bump in the road.

There is something to be gained from each struggle. Nature perfectly models this with butterflies and baby chicks. A butterfly pushing out of its chrysalis would never be able to fly if someone helped pry open its cocoon.

Similarly, a baby chick may not survive or thrive without  the necessary exertion of breaking out of its shell. Each chick is specifically equipped for this purpose, with an "egg tooth" on its beak for cracking the shell that disappears in due time.

Our role is simply to validate and support a child (or any loved one) through the struggle, until he or she believes they will be okay. Henry Ford wisely said, "Whether you believe you can do a thing or not, you are right."

Asking the question, "Will you be okay?" allows a child to decide that he or she is resilient; able to recover from setbacks or suffering, limits or labels, differences or diagnoses. It offers our child the opportunity to believe in his or her capacity for endurance, growth, and progression.

For Jonathan, the experience of being rejected helped him develop compassion for others who were excluded. When asked if he would be okay, Jonathan said, "Yes. I like making new friends, anyway." By completing the validation cycle, Jonathan was able to heal a hurt and identify a strength he possessed.

In most circumstances, once you have completed the previous four steps, the answer to the question, "Will you be okay?" is usually, "Yes," or, "I think so."

A negative response may signal a need to go to a deeper level. This can be reached by repeating the Validation Hero Sequence, or applying the "Treating Trauma and Emotional Drama" tools taught in Chapters 13-18.

Like training wheels on our child's emotional bicycle, we provide stability until our child can apply this validation cycle themselves.

After discovering the relief emotional first aid offers, when noticing a situation that has caused wounding, our child will now have the recipe to build a Hero Slider on their own.

Offering a **self-validation hero recipe,** with slightly altered "bun" statements, our child will use the same winning ingredients sandwiched inside, as outlined below:

Initially, our child may require our support and validation to fully discharge stressful or painful emotions. With time and practice, the emotional resilience skill of learning to identify feelings, and ask for what is needed, empowers a child to discover solutions. In addition, this recipe allows children to develop confidence for facing future challenges.

While we can't rescue our child from every hurtful situation, we represent a reassuring resource to encourage facing feelings, seeking support, and bouncing back.

The Validation Hero Recipe sparks clarity, conversation, and connection central to healthy emotional relationships and secure attachment. As we foster emotional resilience through validation, we inspire willingness for our child to trust, and try again.

Note:

The Validation Hero Recipe can be applied to conversations when communicating with adults, as well. We've all experienced chatting with people who, like a playlist repeating one song, drone on and on about their problems to anyone who's willing to listen--and even to those who are unwilling! What they are seeking is validation.

You'll be surprised how asking, "What's the worst part?" helps an individual focus on what is really bothering them. Inviting someone to identify suppressed emotions by asking, "How do you feel?" often allows them to feel enough support to face and process uncomfortable feelings.

Chapter 6: Validation "Condiments"

"The world's battlefields have been in the heart chiefly; more heroism has been displayed in the household, and the closet, than on the most memorable battlefields in history."
- Henry Ward Beecher

Validation is not just for big upheavals and hurts, but also for everyday discomfort and demands. For example, when our child comes home from school complaining about homework or tests, we can choose how to respond. We can compare their difficulty to what we remember enduring as a child (*walking to and from school through the snow, uphill, both ways*). We can dismiss their burden with a, "Suck it up, Buttercup," or some similar slam. Or, we can simply acknowledge that some aspects of life are less than ideal. Which one builds connection and trust?

Make a mental list of questions and validating phrases that invite conversation to use when a child complains, criticizes, or carps. While none of these questions change the circumstances, they do help a child feel heard and understood, allowing them to shrug off the situation, or lighten the load.

We can start a conversation with a comment such as, "Looks like you've had a rough day." Depending on the level of openness developed through past validation, a child will respond with a story or a shrug. Once you get a child to share what is bothering him or her, you can examine the pieces together.

Imagine a child's account of what happened like dumping out a puzzle or a Lego set on a table. We can help a child sort through the light and dark pieces, or look for similar shapes, by asking questions.

**We ask questions to determine
what is happening in our child's heart.**

The first question which needs to be asked is, "Are you just looking to vent, or do you want help looking at the pieces?" Sometimes a child simply needs to give voice to frustrations or challenges, and have someone validate how it made him or her feel. Other times, a child may be stuck, and need help examining each part to discover:

1) His or her role in whatever happened
2) Potential lessons to be learned
3) Strengths to be developed or abilities to be nurtured

Only after these items have been unpacked and pieced together would we offer our input.

**It's about asking the right questions;
our child has all of the answers!**

Just as a Hero Sandwich is better with condiments, our Validation Hero Recipe is enhanced with better questions and comments.

Questions which invite feeling conversations:

- How long have you been feeling this way?
- Are there other feelings besides the emotion you just shared?
- What would make you feel safe to open up to me?
- Can you pick three "feeling faces" or emotion words to describe how you are feeling?
- On a scale of 1 to 10, how intense is this feeling?
- Can you think of a time you felt this feeling before?
- Where do you feel that feeling in your body right now?
- If that part of your body could talk, what would it want to say?
- If that feeling had a color or a shape, what would it be?
- What do you wish would happen now?

Whatever the issue, we want to help our child develop emotional awareness by asking, "Because 'X' happened, how do you feel?"

Validating phrases (which must be spoken with *genuine* empathy):

- I'll bet . . . (that was hard, difficult, hurtful, etc.).
- Oh, wow!
- Really?
- That stinks . . .
- Tell me more; I want to really understand . . .
- That's tough . . .
- Oh, no!
- That sounds rough . . .
- I would probably feel the same way if that happened to me.
- I can see why you feel . . . (angry, upset, betrayed, etc.)

Mirroring Statements:

- What I hear you saying is _____.
- So, you are feeling _____, because _____.
- From what happened, you think _____, and are feeling _____. Is that right?

Perhaps the biggest challenge is
to ask more than you tell.

During times of distress, we must allow the story to unfold as our child tells it at his or her own pace. As parents, one of the biggest hurdles to communication is our desire to rush to resolve, suggest solutions, or control conflicts.

Instead, we need to become comfortable waiting in the silence for our child to verbalize thoughts and feelings to develop emotional self-awareness skills. Patience is required to do the opposite of what often comes naturally, and to instead take time to just listen.

Listening without interruption allows the focus to stay on our child's perception of the truth, even if we see things differently. We must be careful to ask questions that promote understanding, not our own opinion. Validation must be a judgment-free zone where we allow our child to feel *any* feeling.

Avoid invalidating comments:

In his book, *When Hope Is Not Enough*, Bon Dobbs suggests when seeking to validate someone, it's important not to fall into any of the following competitive, judgmental, or shaming-type statements below:

❖ Trying to one-up: "Oh, you think you have it bad . . ."

❖ Making it about you: "I hated it when that happened to me . . ."

❖ Telling them how they should feel or act: "You should feel . . . (thankful, excited, ashamed of yourself . . .)"

❖ Trying to give them advice: "What you really *should* do is . . ."

❖ Trying to solve their problem: "I'm going to call that girl's parents and . . ."

❖ Cheerleading (there is a time for this, but not now): "I know you can do it . . ."

❖ Making judgmental statements: "What you did was wrong . . ." or, "You are too sensitive . . ."

❖ Making "life" statements: "Well, life's *not* fair . . ."

❖ Making "revisionist" or "corrective" statements: "If only you had . . ."

❖ Making it about your feelings: "How do you think that makes *me* feel?"

❖ Making "character" assessments: "You're too sensitive . . ."

❖ Rationalizing another person's behavior: "Maybe they were just . . ." or, "You just took it wrong . . ."

❖ Using reason or "the facts": "That's not what actually happened . . ."

❖ Using "always" or "never" statements: "You *always* get yourself into these situations . . ."

❖ Comparing the person to someone else: "Why can't you be like your sister?"

❖ Name calling the person: "You're nuts. . . " or, "You're being such a baby . . ."

❖ Advising to cut ties or ignore the situation: "Just ignore him . . ."   (Dobbs, 2015).

Combining active listening with comforting words and touch will enhance validation and relief.

Body Language:

When emotions are present, that is the time to talk. We must immediately turn off the TV, put down our phone, or pull into a parking lot to be fully present for our child.

Children hear not only the words we say, but also pick up cues based on body language: our tone of voice, facial expressions, and level of attention. Our child will sense whether he or she has our full attention, or not.

How we position our body can encourage openness. Consider dropping down to a child's eye level rather than talking down to them. Turning toward a child, then making appropriate physical contact such as: holding a hand, hugging, cuddling close, or placing your hand on a knee or a back will signal an outward show of support.

Physical touch can fill the uncomfortable gap of silence that often exists while our child considers answers to our questions, or processes what has happened. Hugs always help!

Psychotherapist, Virginia Satir, stated, "We need 4 hugs a day for survival. We need 8 hugs a day for maintenance. We need 12 hugs a day for growth" (Satir, 2014). According to *The Happiness Project*, hugs need to be held for at least six seconds to trigger the cascade of happiness hormones.

The process of feeling and freely expressing emotions allows our child to create powerful positive conversations, generate secure attachment patterns, and facilitate emotional resilience.

Chapter 7: Nevertheless . . .
Everyday Validation & Limits

"Call them rules, call them limits, good ones . . .
are an expression of loving concern."
- Fred Rogers

It's only natural that children will test rules, boundaries, and limits. Like the Velociraptors in the movie, *Jurassic Park*, a child will constantly be "checking the fence" for any weaknesses.

Parenting research confirms that children do better with limits and structure. Through regular routines for bedtimes, chores, family dinners, and accountability for academics, a predictable pattern helps our child feel safe and know what is expected.

Parenting expert, Lisa Damour, PhD, suggests that too much unstructured time, along with lack of supervision, creates opportunities for trouble. Things tend to go wrong when opportunity and temptation come together.

In order to best protect our child, we need to consider his or her approach to risk. Dr. Damour counsels, "The best predictor of future behavior is past behavior."

Children - especially teens - tend to evaluate risky behavior based on two factors: the chance they will get caught, or the chance that they will get hurt. Should our child show the first attitude, we will want to set a securely defined perimeter using clear expectations and consequences (Damour, 2016).

"Be a thermostat, not a thermometer" (Ailes, 1988).

Thermometers are reactive, reflecting what's happening around them. Thermostats regulate the temperature by making small adjustments to cool or heat a room. Whether coping with a child's emotional crisis or enforcing rules and boundaries, keeping our cool is essential.

When a situation is hot, thermometer parents heat up too, reacting to what a child has done or experienced. Under tension, this type of parent loses their cool, becoming critical, demanding, impatient, and angry.

Our reaction can trigger fear in a child. "People who are fearful may *say* and *do* what is right, but they do not *feel* the right things. They often feel helpless and resentful, even angry. Over time, these feelings lead to mistrust, defiance, and even rebellion" (Uchtdorf, 2017).

Basically, the only difference between giving our child consequences or punishment is **our** emotional state. Often, our anger rises when a child's choices annoy, inconvenience, or embarrass us. Children need to be loved and taught, but when we lecture with anger or attack, all they feel is: "I'm unsafe, unworthy, or unlovable."

In contrast to thermometers, thermostat parents regulate the environment by setting the desired emotional temperature of the home, and actively adjusting to the needs of those nearby. No matter the situation, thermostat parents focus on restoring balance.

Should a child begin whining or acting out to get his or her way, seeing the behavior as a signal of an unmet need activates our empathy instead of our anger. Perhaps the child is simply tired, hungry, worried, or feeling powerless.

Whatever the cause, our correction needs to come in a coaching mode versus a referee style (*although, we've all seen plenty of coaches who act like referees and point out every mistake, instead of patiently teaching desired skills and actions*). We want to celebrate even imperfect attempts or incremental improvement.

When my children took piano lessons, their teacher, Mr. Burkholder, would listen as they played the assigned piece of music they had practiced for the week. Instead of pointing out  all of the inevitable mistakes in notes or timing, he would select a few measures of the song and say, "Let's fix this." There was no judgment, anger, or criticism; just a calm invitation to make specific improvements in a particular place.

Sometimes, our child will protest about an assignment, chore, or task that needs to be done, despite the discomfort negative consequences cause them. We may ask our child to clean the bathroom, take out the trash, or practice the piano, and be met with excuses about how much homework is waiting, or the desire to finish a video game campaign.

We let our child know we truly care about their feelings as we confirm that their responses are reasonable, while still requiring compliance. In each case, sympathetic validation paves the way to our desired action when we add a pivotal adverb: "Nevertheless . . ."

"Nevertheless" means:
"In spite of that . . ." or
"Despite a situation or a comment."

"Nevertheless . . ." works like this:

> Parent: *"It's time to take out the trash."*
>
> Child: *"Can't I just finish this game? It's really important!"*
>
> Parent: *"I'm sure it is important . . . **nevertheless,** it's time to take out the trash."*
>
> Child: *"Why can't I do it later?"*
>
> Parent: *"I understand you don't want to be interrupted . . . **nevertheless,** it's time to take out the trash. Now, please."*

> Child: *"You are ruining my game! It's so frustrating."*
>
> Parent: *"I'm sure you feel frustrated your game is being ruined . . . **nevertheless,** take out the trash right now."*

The key is to keep our emotional response neutral and focus on the request.

Speaking fewer words from this point onward is a better way to avoid arguments, and keep your cool. Should a child's protests continue, simply choose one word to repeat until he or she gets the message that the request requires immediate action.

In this case, we could simply say, "Trash," or, "Trash now, please," until our child complies. We can then thank him or her for cooperating, even if it wasn't the initial response.

Two critical elements when applying consequences:

1) Keep Calm.

Administer any and all consequences from a neutral emotional state, like a police officer giving a ticket. Keep your face neutral and your tone dispassionate. Simply stated, "A rule was broken and now you will pay the fine."

2) Carry On.

Be sure to consistently carry the consequence to completion. When we fail to follow through, we teach children that they can *sometimes* escape taking responsibility for their actions.

At the heart of behaviorism, intermittent reinforcement happens when a punishment (or reward) is *not* administered every time. This increases the likelihood a behavior will continue. Like gambling, even if you don't win every time, the chance that you might win conditions a habitual response.

Giving a threat or a promise without following through undermines our credibility, and erodes a child's ability to trust in our word. Conversely, when we are calm and consistent *every time* with promised consequences (positive or negative), our child will be certain of the outcome generated by his or her choices.

**Using the pivotal word, "nevertheless,"
along with validation, is helpful
when communicating consequences.**

Should a child complain or argue about the consequences, we continue to express empathetic validation (*"I'm sorry you feel that way,"* or, *"I'm sorry you broke a family rule . . ."*), along with "nevertheless" (*". . . nevertheless, you have lost privileges and/or received extra chores"*).

For example, imagine your child comes home after curfew. At this point, you can express love or disapproval, but not both. Recognizing your emotions are at a boiling point, ideally, you would curb your anger and lovingly express, "Son, I'm glad you're home safe . . . **nevertheless,** we will need to discuss your curfew tomorrow."

Later, when emotions are calm, you can apply validation with love while teaching accountability, saying, "**I'm sorry** you broke your curfew last night . . . **nevertheless,** you are responsible for the choice you made. As we previously agreed, the consequence will be _____."

Hopefully, you have already discussed what a fair consequence for failure to comply with the curfew would be. If not, this would be a good time to ask your child's opinion to determine a reasonable result.

Natural Consequences

Discipline is not about timeouts, revoking privileges, or coercing compliance through fear. Jane Nelson, EdD, author of the *Positive Discipline* series, states, "Kids don't learn when they're feeling threatened."

Instead, we want to provide logical or natural consequences. Dr. Nelson suggests three R's for determining discipline: the consequence should be *related*, *respectful*, and *reasonable*. This approach allows a child to learn from his or her mistakes, instead of simply being punished (Nelson, 2006).

One of my favorite parenting programs is, "Love and Logic." The "love" piece emphasizes that because we love our child, we are willing to set and enforce limits, and will do so with empathy. The "logic" part happens when our child can make decisions or minor mistakes with logical consequences, and hopefully determine that better decisions make a better life (Cline, 2006).

Showing sincere compassion - while maintaining boundaries and setting limits - creates secure emotional attachment with our children.

Setting Limits

When children feel strong negative emotions, they may express them with dysfunctional behaviors such as yelling, hitting, or other tantrum-type actions. The feelings are not the problem, the uncontrolled reactions are.

We can use validation, while setting limits, to ensure our child learns how to act in the face of upsetting feelings. Be as specific as possible when identifying the unwanted behavior, then set the desired boundary. Use an unruffled response such as, "**I'm sorry** you feel angry . . . **nevertheless,** it is not okay to throw things, hit others, or call people names."

It's important that we separate behavior from identity. When a child receives a bad grade at school, they may have failed the test, but they are not a failure. If our child refuses to share a toy, they are *acting* selfish, but should not be labeled as "selfish." As a parent, we need to label the behavior, not our child.

Simply state the situation and the correct course for remedy. For example, "Andy, you are keeping all the cars. Please pick out something Ben can play with." Or, "Devin, your chore was to be done before free time. Please turn off the TV now and unload the dishwasher."

Additionally, it may be helpful to calmly let the child know that you recognized signs of dissatisfaction or distress expressed, and clarify which part is not acceptable. You might say, "I noticed you gave a huge sigh and rolled your eyes when I asked you to set the table. Let's try that again. This time, when I ask you to help, please look me in the eye, say, 'Okay,' and get up from the couch."

Clearly identify desired behavior with requests such as:

- "In the future, please use your words instead of your hands."
- "Next time, ask for help."
- "Please apologize, and after a five-minute timeout, you can join us to have a snack."

No matter a child's response, we can validate the thought or feeling expressed using "nevertheless" to bridge the gap to desired action.

Validation encourages cooperation

Using validation--while keeping our emotional cool--encourages cooperation with younger children as well. Imagine you are at the park, and have given your child a "five-minute warning" that it will be time to go home. When the five minutes have passed, your child ignores your call and keeps playing.

At this point, you can respond with frustration and anger, grabbing your child by the arm and dragging him or her across the park, *OR*, you can get down on their level, make eye contact, and apply validation.

Begin by saying: "I can see you are having fun and want to play longer . . . ***nevertheless,*** it's time to go right now."

Should a tantrum or physical resistance start, the **Validation Hero Recipe** can be applied:

I'm sorry . . . you don't want to stop playing. It has been so much fun!

W **What's the <u>worst</u> part about having to leave now?**

A child might reply that he/she is almost finished building a castle, or didn't have a chance to play on the swings. It could be that there is a friend at the playground. Whatever the feedback, it helps us understand why our child is upset.

I **<u>Identify</u>. How do you feel?**

Negative emotions are generated when a need is left unmet. Don't miss this opportunity to help a child identify and name what he or she is feeling in that moment, so you can validate the emotion. Once an emotion is named, we validate it with words, such as, "I can see why you would feel sad to leave your friend," or, "I'm sure you feel frustrated to leave before your castle is finished."

N **What do you <u>need</u> to make it better?**

We encourage cooperation through choice. A child might say they need five more minutes to finish building their castle, or ask for a push on the swings for a few minutes. They might ask if the friend can come over, or if they can plan a future play date.

When possible, we want to honor and support our child's request.

If time doesn't allow for any of these options, we can still validate the problem-solving solutions suggested with a hug and say, "I wish that we had time for that today." We can then offer a compromise or promised incentive to invite cooperation, such as, "Maybe we can invite your friend over to play after school on Monday," or, "Tonight after dinner we can come back to the park," or, "We have time for one last push on the swings before we go."

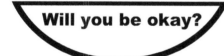

Will you be okay?

Asking this question shows a child that his or her feelings do matter to us, thus reinforcing that emotions are both understandable and controllable. This question also helps a child see the power of choice to internally control his or her emotions and behaviors.

Children raised with emotional validation learn to be open and comfortable with their feelings, can ask for what they

105

need, and develop crucial communication skills necessary to negotiate win-win solutions.

Chapter 8: Getting Through a Rough Patch

"You may encounter many defeats,
but you must not be defeated."
- Maya Angelou

Today, we look for solutions to occur at microwave speed. If our child becomes sick, we rush to the doctor hoping for a prescription to kill off the "bad bugs." With bacterial infections, medication goes immediately to work, and can speed recovery time. However, should the sickness stem from a virus, an antibiotic won't help. Yet, the doctor will often write a prescription to placate a parent.

In a similar fashion, children are being medicated for emotional ailments at an alarming rate. According to the National Alliance on Mental Illness, 1 in 5 youths across the nation have an anxiety or mood disorder. Data from 2014 showed that over *8 MILLION CHILDREN* in the United States are on psychiatric drugs. Prescription drug use is growing, not only among teenagers, but among tens of thousands of preschoolers.

In a September 2010 New York Times article, Duff Wilson wrote about the potential dangers of simply medicating a child, without addressing the underlying issues.

*"**At 18 months**, Kyle Warren started taking a daily antipsychotic drug on the orders of a pediatrician trying to quell the boy's severe temper tantrums. '**Within five minutes** of sitting with him, he looked at me and said, "He has autism, there's no doubt about it,"' Ms. Warren said.*

*Thus began a troubled toddler's journey from one doctor to another, from one diagnosis to another, involving even more drugs. Autism, bipolar disorder, hyperactivity, insomnia, oppositional defiant disorder. The boy's daily pill regimen multiplied: the antipsychotic Risperdal, the antidepressant Prozac, two sleeping medicines and one for attention-deficit disorder. **All by the time he was 3**.*

*He was sedated, drooling and overweight from the side effects of the antipsychotic medicine. Although his mother, Brandy Warren, had been at her 'wit's end' when she resorted to the drug treatment, she began to worry about Kyle's altered personality. '**All I had was a medicated little boy**,' Ms. Warren said. 'I didn't have my son. It's like, you'd look into his eyes and you would just see just blankness . . . I will never, ever let my children be put on these drugs again,' said Ms. Warren, 28, choking back tears. 'I didn't realize what I was doing'"* (Wilson, 2010).

Often, children are labeled with ADHD or Autism as catch-all diagnoses when something is wrong, or a child is different, which can lead to over-diagnosis and consequent over-medicating. A 2008 study found that fewer than half of individuals diagnosed with Bipolar Disorder had the illness, while 5% of those diagnosed with something else actually had Bipolar Disorder (Hendrickson, 2016). Plus, medication is often cheaper for families than paying for counseling.

With this alarming trend, medication dispensed for mental difficulties may simply *mask* problems without mending them.

Psychiatric medications *suppress* natural emotional responses or physical symptoms, which are the body's way of communicating unmet needs. When medicated, children don't learn how to manage life's ups and downs, or make necessary course corrections in behavior and relationships.

Many times, distress or mental illness is triggered by an **inciting event**. Left untreated, an emotional wound may become a pain point or a "thought virus," which festers in the mind.

These corrupting thoughts, coupled with strong emotion, can become beliefs the mind accepts as absolute truth. Generated as a result of real or perceived trauma, unhappy thoughts can have a poisonous effect on the brain.

Like a physical virus, a "thought virus" cannot be cured with medication.

When a child is sick with a virus, it affects the entire body. Similarly, a "thought virus" can cue genuine physical responses from the body. For my daughter, Katie, the belief, "I can be forgotten," tapped into a basic survival instinct, sending her brain into fight/flight/freeze mode.

While Katie believed she wasn't safe to leave the house (because she might be lost or forgotten, again), for her mind, the danger was real. Her body responded just as if there was a lion outside, waiting to pounce.

Never having dealt with mental illness before, it was terrifying to see the torture of her frenzied mind. Any time Katie had to leave home, she was an emotional wreck.

I was baffled as to why that experience of being left behind at the park could generate what seemed like such an exaggerated response. She seemed to have handled the situation perfectly, turning to a trusted adult and asking for help. Yet, her unacknowledged feelings had festered into a sickening "thought virus," producing a program of fear.

Powerless to help my precious daughter, no amount of reassurance could change her belief that she could be forgotten again. Feeling exhausted, helpless, and guilty, I blamed myself for her insecurities and fear. I had no idea where to turn or what to do.

The worst part was that it felt like the burden was all mine. Most meltdowns happened after my husband had already gone to work. I was the one receiving multiple phone calls from her school each day; I was the one managing teacher meetings and school policies. At home, Katie was relaxed and content, so my husband couldn't understand the daily drama I faced. Feeling helpless to fix her worries and having no idea where to look for answers, I feared things were never going to get better.

Finally, deciding I was in over my head, I sought professional help. Trying to schedule appointments with medical doctors and counselors was frustrating, because they were booking appointments weeks out when I needed immediate help.

Once in therapy, the counselor wanted to spend several sessions over multiple weeks "building a relationship of trust." Meanwhile, I was drowning with the burden of daily meltdowns.

Desperate for help, I took Katie to a recommended psychologist who was trained in EMDR. Eye Movement Desensitization and Reprocessing (EMDR) is a psychotherapy treatment designed to alleviate distress associated with traumatic memories by re-living trauma, while focusing on external stimulus. While some have had success with this treatment, we were not so fortunate.

During sessions, Katie was asked to re-live the trauma of being forgotten, over and over, while holding onto electrodes that alternated signals from right to left hands to "desensitize" her psyche to the fear of being forgotten. Like repeatedly watching a sports blunder on a highlight reel, this process was traumatizing for her, while agonizing and guilt-producing for me.

After several weeks with no decrease in fear or symptoms,  the doctor suggested we put Katie on some anti-anxiety medication to "open a window," so we could get inside her mind to defuse the ticking anxiety-bomb there. While not a fan of numbing or masking issues with medication, at this point I was willing to try almost anything if it would help.

Since our counselor was not licensed to prescribe medication, we booked an appointment with the psychiatrist on staff, who we will call Dr. H. When we arrived for Katie's appointment, I was given a four-page assessment to fill out. When the questions progressed to, "Have you ever thought of harming yourself or others?" *I* was the one feeling anxiety. I became very upset that this line of inquiry might put ideas into my daughter's head that she never would have considered on her own. They were asking questions a little girl should never have to worry about.

Already keyed up from the questionnaire, we waited for Dr. H to review the answers, and Katie's file. Then, *without ever having met my daughter*, he breezed into the room announcing, "Your daughter has General Anxiety Disorder, and in order to cope will need to be medicated for the rest of her life."

How could that sentence roll so flippantly off his tongue? The "rest of her life" was a very long time when she was just 10 years old! His diagnosis felt as severe as a lifetime-prison sentence with no hope of parole. To me, his conclusion had the same impact I would have felt if he had strolled in and cheerily announced they were going to have to amputate her leg, but she would only have to limp around . . . for the rest of her life.

Not surprisingly, I burst into tears. His diagnosis dropped like a guillotine, cleaving my heart in two as I watched dreams for my daughter fall away. What were the long-term implications of a lifetime of medication? Would she be able to continue going to school, attend college, get married, and have children? Would we be able to travel without her constant anxiety that the plane might crash, or that she would become separated from us, or could be forgotten . . . again?

Having prior experience with friends taking mental health medications, I realized that finding the right dose could take months--and possibly years. We were no longer talking about just "opening a window" to help her. Plus, what about harmful side-effects from medications, like potential liver or kidney damage, emotional numbness, or suicide?

Looking at my tears, Dr. H. stated in a compassionless tone, "I don't understand why you're so upset. Did you cry when she got glasses?" Indignant at how he could compare prescribing a lifetime course of psychiatric medication with needing glasses, I replied, "Yes, as a matter of fact, I did! Having worn glasses since second grade, I know what it's like to be nearly blind and unable to function without corrective lenses. I think you're understating the impact of your analysis."

In my mind, the doctor's dreadful diagnosis meant not only that my child was broken, but that there was no hope she could ever get better.

Labels can make the verdict bigger than the individual.

Labels are limiters. Names give symptoms power. If a child shows signs of anxiety we want to label the feelings or behaviors without providing a final verdict.

A diagnosis may become a crutch used by a child when things get tough or uncomfortable. Instead of expressing belief that the child can succeed despite difficulties, in some cases, well-meaning but overprotective parents will excuse a child from contact with challenging situations.

Many times, the diagnosis . . .

- ADD/ADHD
- Bipolar Disorder
- General Anxiety Disorder (GAD)
- Chronic Depression
- Borderline Personality Disorder (BPD)
- Autism Spectrum (AS)

. . . becomes not just a label, but an identity.

Titles can have a toxic effect. People describe the child saying, "He's depressed," instead of, "He's showing signs of depression." Or, they might brand a child saying, "She's autistic," as if it's a personality or character flaw. I didn't want Dr H.'s diagnosis to affect the way others viewed Katie, or, more importantly, the way she viewed herself.

With nothing left to be said, we left the doctor's office, a drug prescription in hand, and my heart heavy with defeat. Driving directly to the neighborhood pharmacy, I was told there was a 30-minute wait. Reluctant to have my daughter miss more school, I took her back to class and returned alone to pick up the dreaded prescription.

Arriving at home, I curled into a fetal position on my bed and cried into my pillow. The sadness spilled out of me like water gushing from a broken dam. I had tried to be strong for so many months, thinking we just needed to get through this rough patch and then things would be better. Now, I felt swamped in sadness and despair.

Heartsick, I called my church leader and poured out my anguish over the situation. Knowing his wife had a diagnosed mental illness, I was certain he would understand my pain.

After listening without interruption, he gave me some very wise counsel, saying, "Just because you have that prescription doesn't mean you have to give it to Katie today. Don't do it until you feel right about it. You will be guided to know what to do." The instantaneous relief I felt was like a ray of sunshine breaking through a stormy sky that had threatened destruction.

As I was lying on the bed contemplating his counsel, a stroke of inspiration came to me. Katie knew she was going to be getting a doctor-prescribed pill to help her. What if I switched out the medication with a placebo? Rummaging through the cupboard, I found a multivitamin that my daughter had never seen before, and switched the contents with the prescription inside the pill bottle.

When I brought Katie home from school that day, I explained that this medication was her "Thinking Pill." While it wouldn't change the fearful thoughts or anxiety that might surface, it would give her brain a space to think things through and make a different, calm and comfortable choice. She started taking her "Thinking Pill" that evening.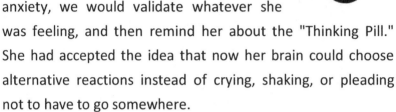

From that day forward, every time Katie would start to show signs of panic, worry, or anxiety, we would validate whatever she was feeling, and then remind her about the "Thinking Pill." She had accepted the idea that now her brain could choose alternative reactions instead of crying, shaking, or pleading not to have to go somewhere.

Together, we would brainstorm about what it would take for her to feel better or safe in that moment, or during upcoming situations. This process allowed her to switch from an emotional state to a thinking state, where she was able to release her negative fears and feelings, and replace them with selected feelings of safety, peace, and hope.

To my complete amazement, the placebo was working. Katie would take her pill in the morning, and leave for school without a fuss. The daily phone calls from school stopped. She could be reasoned with and begin to self-soothe. Within six weeks, Katie said she didn't need to take the pills anymore.

"Tough times don't define you, they refine you."
– Carlos A. Rodriguez

Over the next few months, we continued to validate her fears. Anytime she faced an anxiety-triggering situation, I would suggest she take her "Thinking Pill" for a few days to help her focus on solutions instead of the problems. During this time, I continued to research and discover additional tools to help her foster emotional resilience. After awhile, I only had to ask, "Do you want the Thinking Pill?" and she would reply that she knew what to do to be okay.

Katie is now 22 years old. She went from being unable to leave the house without extreme anxiety, to not only attending but excelling in school. She was a leader of her young women's group, and attended overnight girls' camps in the mountains. Selected as the first female representative of her high school for Idaho Girls State, she stayed on a college campus for a full week, living and participating with complete strangers in uncharted activities.

After graduating from high school, Katie was able to move out of state to attend college. She felt confident walking to and from campus, making new friends, attending activities at untested venues, living independently, and being generally optimistic.

At age 19, she spent 18 months as a church representative, serving a mission in the state of Michigan. This included responsibilities that no one with an untreated anxiety disorder could carry out, including cold-calling by knocking on complete strangers' doors to share a message about Christ, or to give service. She was a leader and a trainer of other female missionaries. During that time, the only contact allowed with family was a phone call on Christmas and Mother's Day, and one weekly e-mail.

Today, Katie is a bright, confident, capable woman, who is successful at anything she decides to do. Recently married and graduated from college, she continues to apply emotional resilience tools to manage whatever challenges come her way.

I'm not sharing all of these things to brag about my daughter's achievements (*although she is pretty amazing*), but to illustrate the power of the mind and of our beliefs. I can't imagine what her life would be like now had we accepted a doctor's diagnosis for a *life-long label* of General Anxiety Disorder, and *lifetime reliance* on emotionally-numbing medication.

A strong personal endorsement for or against a diagnosis can also have a placebo effect.

Interestingly, a Harvard Program in Placebo Studies (PiPS) is studying the effects of fake pills passed off as genuine pharmaceuticals. Researchers are finding that expectations shape our experience. Belief in the healing power of a pill is triggered "not just by fake pharmaceuticals but by the symbols and rituals of healthcare itself," such as the doctor in a white coat, a pill bottle, the label, and the prescription.

Findings indicate that the effects of placebos are not imaginary. After taking a placebo, functional magnetic imaging has captured small changes in the brain indicating neurochemical release, just like with real pharmaceuticals.

Researchers at the PiPS found that **the most important ingredient of the placebo effect turns out to be an *empathetic caregiver*.** "The healing force, or whatever we are going to call it, passes through the placebo, but it helps if it starts with a person, someone who wants you to get better" (Siegel, 2017).

There is real power in a belief. What a person believes about their health or illness is central to how they cope, respond to treatment and evaluate their capacity for healing.

We can encourage a child to drop self-limiting labels by saying, "You don't have that" (ie: "You don't have anxiety. You might *feel* anxious sometimes, but you will be okay." Or, "You don't have depression. It's normal to feel sad or discouraged from time to time"). Repeated exposure to our assurance increases the likelihood our child will believe those assertions (Gilbert, 1993).

Of course, I'm not suggesting that all medications are bad, or that every person could overcome legitimate mental illnesses with a placebo. However, just as caffeine shouldn't be a substitute for a good night's sleep, psychiatric drugs should never be used to simply sedate a child who is causing or having problems.

**Medication ought to be considered a spare tire;
a temporary solution for getting through
a rough patch until real repairs can be made.**

No family member or friend . . . no doctor, therapist, or teacher has the power or right to tell you what is best for your child. Trust your intuition. Seek guidance from God, or a higher power, to find the right tools, information, and individuals to help you help your child. As your child's protector, don't give in to pressure when your heart tells you to take a different path.

Remember, YOU are the expert on your child.

Take a moment and ask yourself what your heart tells you is right or true for your child. What do you know for sure? What questions do you need answered? Use the space below to write down your insights.

Part II: PREPARE

Chapter 9: Leaning Into the Discomfort

"It's he or she who's willing to be the most uncomfortable [that] can rise strong. Leaning into it actually helps you eventually push through."
- Brené Brown

 When my friend Kaira's son was six he smacked his head requiring staples to repair the gash. He asked her if receiving staples would be painful. Kaira honestly replied, "Yes, Son, it's going to hurt, but I'll be right here the whole time holding your hand, and you'll be okay."

To Kaira's surprise the nurse criticized her in front of her son, saying, "You shouldn't scare him like that." Kaira replied, **"I'm not trying to scare him, I'm trying to prepare him."**

Similarly, we can set a child up for success by preparing him or her for emotionally-taxing or emotionally-charged situations. When we reassure our child, "It is normal to feel  scared/nervous/apprehensive/anxious/worried before . . . (*the first day of a new school year/a piano recital/a first date/the big game, or any other concern*) . . . **but you will be okay**," distressing emotions lose their potency.

Part of validation acknowledges that a child is having a hard time, but you believe they can persevere despite the challenge or concern.

Instead of resisting or reassuring, learning to treat an intrusive thought as just a thought can often disrupt its potency.

Recently, a friend reported her struggle to get her elementary-aged son off to school.

Eddy was worried his hair was sticking up. He kept returning to the bathroom, wetting his hand, and pushing the hair down. In frustration, he put his whole head under the faucet, becoming soaked in the process. Mom's reassurance that Eddy's hair was not sticking up couldn't overcome his own belief that it was. Minutes ticked by, and Mom was at her wits' end, knowing that if her son was late to school that would only escalate his anxiety.

Children on the Autism spectrum, those with sensory processing disorders, anxiety, OCD or other mental health challenges, can become stuck in a whirlpool of obsessive thinking. Some thoughts are unreasonable, nonsensical, or even uncontrollable.

While sounding counterintuitive, validation can be used to help overcome fears and worries. In Eddy's case, when he expressed concern that his hair was sticking up, his mom could calmly answer, "Probably."

In this case, the validation sequence acknowledges that although something *MIGHT* happen, the trouble *WON'T* be greater than you can bear, and that you *WILL* be okay.

Each victory over fears and worries builds a confident core to face the next challenge.

Cognitive Behavior Therapy (CBT) suggests overcoming obsessive or intrusive thoughts and fear with "exposures," which means doing things despite discomfort. By validating a child experiencing difficulty, disappointment, or discouragement, we bring our child back to a neutral baseline where better emotions like diligence, daring, and determination can be claimed.

For a timid child, this might be giving a food order directly to a waitress, instead of having a parent order for them. It may look like the child calling to schedule a dentist appointment, or inviting someone new to play after school.

For an anxious child, we can offer a **"when-then"** strategy. For example, during the months my daughter was afraid to leave home, I would kiss the palm of her hand and tell her that **when** she needed comfort while we were apart, **then** she could put that hand up to her cheek and get a kiss from me.

Likewise, we can use a **when-then** strategy to prepare our child for school situations or other new circumstances by teaching, "**When** you feel frustrated (*or any other distressing emotion*), **then** find a grown-up and ask for help." Or, "**When** you start to feel anxious during the test, **then** take a deep breath and repeat in your mind the words, "I am . . . (safe, able, smart and/or winning)."

Self-regulation is like a muscle that gets stronger when regularly flexed.

The struggle is real.

As parents, we face occasional (*or frequent*) power struggles when a child wants something his or her way. Maybe our child wants the red cup over the blue, or to have a sandwich cut into triangles instead of rectangles. While expressing preferences should be allowed, a parent must determine the practicality of accommodating those requests.

For example, children with Sensory Processing Disorder are sensitive to fabrics, tags, and clothing seams. Removing tags or permitting a child to alternate between *two* favorite shirts (though truly preferring one over the other) allows sensitivity to be acknowledged, while still accomplishing the goal of getting dressed. For children with ADD, simply having a chair they can rock back in at school, or putting a piece of Velcro inside a desk for them to touch, can keep them in their seat and minimize disruptions.

Concessions can be made
without compromising compliance.

Not every demand can or should be fulfilled. Children need to understand that they don't live in a me-centric, "I-want-it-now" world, like the character, Veruca in *Willy Wonka and the Chocolate Factory*.

Learning to delay gratification, or the fulfillment of desires, is an essential part of emotional self-regulation. In the late 1960's, psychologist and professor at Stanford University, Walter Mischel, conducted a series of studies on delayed gratification.

Known as the "Marshmallow Experiment," a child would be

offered a choice between a small reward provided immediately, or two small rewards if the child waited while the tester left the room for a short time and then returned. The

reward was often a marshmallow, but sometimes a cookie or a pretzel (Mischel, 2014).

High-delaying children found success, not just by distracting themselves, but by reframing the temptation to a lower emotional temperature. For example, the child would imagine the reward as only a picture, or pretend the marshmallow was simply a puffy cloud.

In follow-up studies, researchers found that children who were able to wait the full 15 minutes for rewards were less likely to have problems with behavior, obesity, or drug addiction by the time they reached high school. Clearly, self-control--with the strength to delay gratification, persevere despite obstacles, and expend effort to achieve goals--is a trait worth cultivating.

Agency - the ability to choose and act for oneself - ought to be encouraged and cultivated.

Some parents decide to let their children choose everything they want to do or not to do. Problems arise when a child decides they don't want to participate in anything that takes effort, or, "doesn't sound fun."

In her book, *The Gifts of Imperfection*, researcher Brené Brown blames the conditioning for "fun, fast, and easy" on our culture (Brown, 2010). Many children develop an entitlement attitude as they come to expect rewards with little effort (a trophy for just showing up), or to be rescued from responsibilities.

Protective and hyper-involved parents can unknowingly create insecurity where a child avoids situations that might otherwise develop coping and competency skills. Instead, parents need to balance validating a child's distress without taking away mildly stressful experiences needed to develop self-reliance.

With younger children, consider giving "either-or" choices, such as: sneakers or sandals, hamburgers or hotdogs, basketball or baseball.

As children mature, offer the opportunity to make choices when the stakes are small, to minimize potentially unpleasant consequences. For example: allowing a child to choose whether or not to take an umbrella when rain is forecast results in a natural consequence of either staying dry, or risking a soaking. Knowledge gained through experience tends to be lasting.

While we hope our child will always make good choices, mistakes will inevitably be made. As parents, this is the time when *our* emotional self-regulation is required. Instead of focusing on the failure, provide connection and calm conversation to facilitate lesson-learning.

Be sure to validate emotions of shame, regret, or unworthiness that a child might feel when a mistake is made to prevent these emotions from becoming an identity-belief, such as, "I am a failure," or, "I am worthless." This lifts the double-weight of both feeling bad, and feeling bad about oneself.

As parents, seek to do less and validate more. Ask yourself what you can *stop* doing for your child that will allow a child to grow. Then, be ready to acknowledge ensuing emotions (such as discouragement or frustration), and offer encouragement to keep going.

Emphasize "becoming" over "doing." Studies show that asking children to be "good helpers" encourages better participation than asking them to help. When praise for positive actions is tied to character, it becomes even more self-motivating.

Emotional resilience doesn't mean protecting a child from uncomfortable or challenging situations.

As a toddler is learning to walk, we *expect* them to fall or fail. No parent is surprised when our child takes a few unsteady steps before dropping down. It would be unthinkable to say, "Oh, looks like my kid's a 'stumbler.' She might as well hang up her walking shoes right now."

Rather, as parents, we find ourselves hunched over, holding our child's fingers so she can experience the thrill of walking *with our support*. We speak encouragement, applaud every attempt, and celebrate even the slightest improvement.

If only every new challenge for our child could be addressed in a similar fashion. Can you imagine the freedom to try and fail . . . and try again?

Emotional 911: For Parents

Last summer, at Women's Aha! Camp, I participated in a high ropes course where we had to walk across a tightrope cable 30 feet in the air. The impossible became possible with the security of a safety harness, locking belay, and attached ropes.

When I lost my balance, I was protected from a long drop and sudden stop by this safety equipment. More importantly, when I lost my nerve, encouraging words from friends below helped me complete the challenge.

Emotional Safety Net

We are sometimes quick to give space for learning and skill development in the physical arena, like when our child is learning to ride a bike or play catch. Emotionally, however, we often leave our child floundering, or worse, cowering in shame when their action doesn't meet our expectations.

Instead, our supportive validation can offer our child confidence to attempt new experiences, while trusting the security of an emotional safety net. As we promote a growth mindset, our child can freely try, feeling confident that they can rise each time they fall.

Praising effort over end results encourages a child to develop "grit" - the determination and perseverance necessary for personal growth.

Develop Grit.

In his book, *Outliers*, Malcolm Gladwell suggested that 10,000 hours of "deliberate practice" are needed to master a new skill set; anything from sports and music to computer programming. However, new research suggests that 10,000 hours of **"deliberate experimentation"** provide greater opportunity for success in any field (Simmons, 2017).

Having a sense of purpose is a key pillar of grit, yet, Duckworth recommends young children "sample widely" activities and sports, exploring a variety of interests to find their passion (Duckworth, 2016).

Just as Thomas Edison tried 1,000 times to develop the light bulb, a child needs space, time, and support to explore interests and discover personal strengths. Encouraging a child to ask questions and make lists of what they want to learn, or places they want to explore, promotes creativity and sparks joy.

Show a child success stories of individuals who have confronted and overcome challenges. Many athletes, actors and musicians are speaking up about experiencing anxiety and depression. Their vulnerability helps remove the stigma and shame of struggle. This helps children feel like they are not alone, and can push forward despite fears.

Be on the lookout for mentors and role models who can inspire from a distance or actively participate in nurturing a child's passions and talents. It's not about winning or losing; it's about being in the game.

Convinced grit can be cultivated, researcher Angela Duckworth suggests those with grit have four traits in abundance:

    a) resilience

    b) willingness to engage in deliberate practice

    c) passion, and

    d) a worthwhile goal

> If you want to find how your child ranks on the grit scale, take Duckworth's test at http://angeladuckworth.com/grit-scale.

Day by day, the emotional support we show encourages our child to be excited--even in failure--about what was learned and apply that knowledge when facing the next challenge.

If we stop seeking to prevent discomfort, and instead, help our child face it, the fight fades away.

Accepting unhappiness, worry, or fear doesn't mean resigning to wallowing in those emotions. Instead, it opens a space to discover the relief of acknowledging the present difficulty.

When our child is in a heightened emotional state, we can invite him or her to dip a toe into the discomfort. **Naming the fear or feeling, and trusting it is *always* fleeting and will pass, provides buoyancy to a child drowning in emotion.** No longer thrashing in the water, our child can finally learn how to float.

Chapter 10: The Body-Mind Connection

"Inaction breeds doubt and fear.
Action breeds confidence and courage."
– W. Clement Stone

When a child is overwhelmed with feelings, it's almost as if he or she becomes temporarily detached, forgetting about the body. Instead of floundering, we can invite a child to immediately do something physical. He or she can march or jump in place, run up and down the stairs, or pretend to walk  across a tightrope toe-to-toe, with arms extended. Where possible, encourage a child to go outside and walk or play for a few minutes. Invite a child to keep moving until a shift is felt in his or her mind, and a reconnection is felt with the body.

For children prone to temper tantrums, invite them to sit and hold their toes. They can do this directly, or cross hands to hold feet on opposite sides of the body. If a child will allow, parents can hold the toes for a few minutes of connection.

Physical movement is one vital way we can help our child reconnect with the body. Grounding themselves to the present moment and their surroundings, children can regain the power of choice. Then, applying the Validation Hero Recipe, we can invite our child to notice what he or she needs to be okay.

Certain practices employ emotional healing tools utilizing a body-mind connection.

Teaching a child to engage in deliberate physical action can help him or her shift from negative to positive emotions.

 **Four excellent choices which offer physical action to alter mental duress are: Power Poses, Brain Gym®, Jin Shin Jyutsu®, and Laughter Yoga.**

POWER POSES

Have you ever wondered why superheroes are so popular with children? Is it the ability to leap tall buildings in a single bound, shoot webs from wrists, or is it the cool costume?

Many think the clout is in the cape, but perhaps the real power comes from the pose. You know the one--hands on hips, chest out, chin up--the posture that says, "I've got this! I can handle anything that comes my way."

Science now shows supportive brain chemicals are released through intentional body positioning. Amy Cuddy, a researcher at Harvard University, and her team have identified that holding a "high power" body position for as little as *two minutes* can increase testosterone (boosting confidence) and decrease cortisol (reducing stress) by as much as 25%.

Body position affects how we think and feel about ourselves. When stressed or anxious, the body naturally curls inward, becoming smaller to protect vital organs. "Low-power" positions involve folding the body, crossing arms or legs, and taking up less space. Conversely, deliberately holding "high power," open and expansive postures benefit children and adults alike.

"Power posing" provides a two-minute supercharge, potentially changing not only how children feel inside, but how they are perceived, as well.

So, that hands-on-the-hips, "Wonder Woman," or superhero pose literally signals the brain to release helpful hormones, which increase belief in our ability to succeed. Happily, this pose works for either gender.

www.clipartxtras.com

Another high-power position is the "Victory" pose: chin up, fists closed with hands thrown triumphantly in the air in the shape of the letter "V." This energizing stance is so innately wired into the human body, that even people blind from birth make this gesture when winning.

Invite a child to practice posing in the mirror before a big test or a game. Encourage him or her to start the day with both arms to the sky in a big "V"-stretch. By pre-loading positive emotions *before* facing everyday stressful situations – from school to recitals, from talks to sporting events – we improve a child's probability of success.

As Amy Cuddy reports, in her TED Talk, "Our bodies change our minds, and our minds change our behavior, and our behavior changes our outcomes" (Cuddy, 2012).

Power poses may be just the stimuli needed to help our child soar . . . cape optional.

BRAIN GYM®

The Brain Gym method suggests up to 26 exercises we can do with a child to balance the brain, and reactivate the body's healing wisdom. It's not necessary to do them all collectively.

Experiment and choose a few as your go-to grounding options. These easy body movements take just minutes, and may increase attention, improve mood, and lessen anxiety.

Google "Brain Gym" to locate several YouTube videos, websites and books with more information and pictures. The article, *Top 10 Simple Brain Gym Exercises And Its Benefits,* suggests a few exercises to get you started:

- Cross Crawl – alternate touching left hand to right knee and right hand to left knee, as if marching. You can also touch opposite elbows to knees. Do for two to three minutes, either standing in place or while moving around the room.

- Belly Breathing – place hands on your stomach; exhale through the mouth in short puffs, as if trying to keep a feather in the air, until your lungs feel empty. Then, inhale deeply, filling yourself like a balloon beneath your hands. Repeat this cycle for three or more breaths.

- Brain Buttons - There are two hollow areas under your collarbone. Position one hand with its index finger and thumb widely spaced like a large "L". Gently pulse these indentations with one hand for a minute or two while resting your other hand over your navel..

- Thinking Cap – Use your thumb and index finger to unroll the outer part of the upper earlobe. Slide fingers down the earlobe and gently pull. Repeat three times.

- Neck Rolls - Drop your head forward and relax your shoulders. While breathing, close your eyes and easily roll your head from side to side 4-5 times.

- Energy Yawn – as you begin to yawn, lightly press the fingertips of each hand against any tight spots on the jaw near the ears. Make a deep yawning sound while gently massaging away any tension. Repeat three times.

- Think of an "X" - Close your eyes and visualize the letter X. Notice how your eyes co-ordinate to connect right, left, upper and lower visual fields around a point of focus.

- Hook-Ups – Sit or stand with the right leg crossed over the left at the ankles. Place your right wrist over the left, and curl your hands inward so the fingers interlock. Rotate the wrists so the fingers are toward the body, and elbows are pointed outward, hands pulled toward the chest. Hold for a few minutes while breathing deeply and slowly.

- Lazy Eights - Extend your arm straight out in front of you, equal to your shoulder level. With your thumb pointing toward the ceiling, slowly and smoothly trace the shape of a large figure 8. While drawing the 8, try to focus your eyes on the thumb (M, 2017).

Jin Shin Jyutsu®

Jin Shin Jyutsu is a Japanese healing art for balancing the mind, body and spirit using your own hands. The body has energy pathways that can become blocked or shorted out by stressful experiences, causing pain, discomfort, or other symptoms. Teaching a child to breathe deeply while holding specific fingers can clear the "traffic jam," and activate the body's natural ability to soothe and heal.

Mary Burmeister offers a wonderful introduction to the art of Jin Shin Jyutsu in her children's book, *Fun with Happy Hands* (Burmeister, 1988). Training a child to choose which finger needs to be held triggers evaluation of what emotion is causing distress. This fosters confidence to face and manage feelings during challenging situations.

Jin Shin Jyutsu addresses five major feelings—or repetitive patterns of thought—which can be helped by gently holding specific fingers. Simultaneously, each finger corresponds with the spine and specific organs in the body.

The attitudes and respective fingers are:

- Worry (thumb)
- Fear (index)
- Anger (middle)
- Sadness (ring)
- Trying-to or "efforting" (pinky)

You can remember the order starting with the thumb by thinking this method "**works fast.**" W.F.A.S.T = worry, fear, anger, sadness, trying-to.

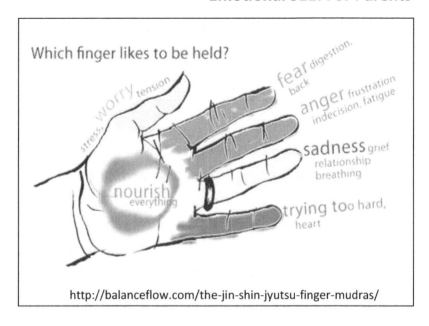

Which finger likes to be held?

worry tension

stress,

fear digestion,

back

anger frustration

indecision, fatigue

sadness grief
relationship
breathing

nourish
everything

trying too hard,
heart

http://balanceflow.com/the-jin-shin-jyutsu-finger-mudras/

Laughter Yoga

Almost everyone has heard the expression, "Laughter is the best medicine," but studies are proving measureable emotional benefits derived from laughing. The ability to maintain a sense of humor and laugh, especially before or after an anxiety-producing situation, acts as a positive coping mechanism.

Laughter Yoga combines laughter-inducing, interactive bodily exercises with deep centering breathing and stretching. Formulated on the concept that our bodies can't tell the difference between real and fake laughter, both kinds of laughs generate the same beneficial results.

Search for Laughter Yoga lists on the Internet, videos posted on YouTube, or a local class. Then invite your child to join you in giggle-producing antics as you imagine laying eggs

 like a chicken, jumping like a frog, tip-toeing across hot sand, mixing milkshakes, pretending everything you touch gives a shock of static electricity, or laughing through the vowel alphabet.

The laughter becomes real and contagious as you keep eye contact while performing laughter yoga frolics together, singing funny songs or improvising dance routines. Results show laughter reduces anxiety depression and stress hormone production, and improves sleep, mood (including optimism and self-esteem) and immune cell creation (Rosenfeld, 2018).

In the end, the best solution is the one that offers relief for you and your child.

No two children are alike. Different personality types and special needs or situations will determine which practice will provide the level of emotional first aid required.

Any of these methods can bring a child back to a place of power. When feeling out of control, choosing an intentional physical motion may help a child cope with difficult situations, relieve everyday life stress and balance emotions.

Again, trust your instincts, and invite your child to participate in the process of applying emotional healing tools to find relief. Suggesting solutions to reconnect with the body helps a child switch from thinking (or obsessing) mode into feeling mode where healing happens.

Chapter 11: Reservoirs of Resilience

"The struggle you are in today is developing the strength you need for tomorrow."
- Robert Tew

My friend, Cynthia, was born with a green thumb. Like the love a mother gives her children, she carefully nurtures the tender seedlings in her greenhouse. Offering controlled temperature and protection from the elements, the greenhouse would seemingly create a perfect environment for optimum growth.

Yet, interestingly, Cynthia has found that the plants won't develop the *RESILIENCE* necessary to thrive unless she positions a fan to blow across the fragile sprouts. The resulting breeze provides just enough stress to strengthen roots and foster hardiness for future transplanting.

Similarly, as parents, it's easy to want to control our child's environment, protecting him or her from any possible discomfort, distress, or harm. However, research suggests that **exposure to moderate stress levels tends to make people stronger and better able to manage future stress.**

A 2010 study led by Dr. Mark D. Seery at UCLA, found that "people with a history of *some* lifetime adversity reported better mental health and well-being outcomes than not only people with a high history of adversity, but also than people with no history of adversity." Not surprisingly, people with lots of lifetime trauma had the worst mental and physical health. Yet, **those who experienced *some* life challenges were the least affected by recent, stressful life incidents."** (Seery, 2010). The researchers determined:

> **"*In moderation*, whatever does not kill us may indeed make us stronger."**

Intentional Resilience Building

Before our child begins attending school we preemptively inoculate them against illness. When given a vaccine, the body is capable of successfully fighting this tiny amount of bacteria or virus to become immunized against future disease. Likewise, as parents we can stimulate our child's emotional resilience with immunizing activities designed to help fight off future duress.

Happiness in families is most likely achieved when parents provide opportunities for social, physical, emotional and spiritual growth in a nurturing and loving environment. Applying intentional parenting principles, like teaching a child to work, play, learn and serve, are the "what" of resilience building. The "how" relies on individual family practices based on these core principles.

The following are suggested practices to strengthen the family - *whatever shape, size or configuration your family happens to be* - and to build reservoirs of resilience in a child.

♥ **Work Hard**

- Give a child chores and responsibilities appropriate for age, ability, and maturity. Although it's often "easier" to do things yourself, allow a child to master valuable housekeeping and life skills.
- School is a child's work. Teach accountability for school lunches, gym clothes, and musical instruments, as well as completing and returning homework.
- When and where possible, encourage employment, even if that means encouraging children or teens to start their own business. From lemonade stands to window washing, children's confidence grows as they develop a personal work ethic.
- Find opportunities for service in your neighborhood, church, or community to help a child focus outside of him or herself. JustServe.org provides a wonderful online resource to discover local needs by zip code.

> *Want Confident Teens? Encourage Them to Help Strangers.*
>
> *A Flourishing Families Project study by Professor Laura Padeilla-Walker, shows children and teens that help people they don't know see a bigger boost in self-esteem than helping family or friends.*
>
> *Research indicates helping with humanitarian projects or choosing a way to serve in their community increases the feeling they can effect change.*
>
> *When children and adolescents directly see the benefit of helping others, they see themselves as more capable, and develop confidence to get out of their comfort zone.*
>
> *Helping people who aren't related can start the growth of the empathy muscle, increase gratitude, and help youth focus less on their own problems (Collins, 2017).*

❤ **Play Hard**

In our family we like to say, "Work hard, play harder." Make playing with your child(ren) a priority.

- Spend at least part of one day each week involved in a family recreational activity.
- Exercise elevates mood. Play sports together, sign up for "fun runs," get outdoors for a hike, bike, ski, or swim.
- Spending time in nature boosts both mental and physical health. Explore zoos, museums, and historical sites. Plan family road trips and vacations together.

♥ **Increase "Face" Time**

- Set family rules such as "no electronics at meals."
- Create bedtime rituals of stories and songs.
- Take occasional social media fasts, limit screen time, or have regular electronic-free days.
- Skype or Smartphone chat with extended family.
- Adopt a "grandparent," or bake and take cookies to a neighbor.
- Encourage real relationships over virtual ones.

♥ **Family Mealtimes**

Make sitting down together for family mealtime a daily event. Evidence suggests that eating family meals at home is the strongest predictor of children's academic achievement and psychological adjustment.

The simple act of preparing a meal and enjoying it together provides better nutrition and opportunities to build stronger relationships. Family mealtimes have been shown to be a safeguard against a child's drinking, smoking, or using drugs.

Think of mealtime as a celebration.

"After our whole family has survived another day, with all of its ups and downs, we come together in the evening and celebrate together. We don't have to wait for birthdays or holidays to be happy together.

Life is short. It doesn't matter that we're eating macaroni and cheese with mismatched forks. What does matter is that we make mealtime a relaxed and enjoyable time together" (Baadsgaard, 1998).

💜 **Confident Communication**

- Teach and model interest in others by initiating conversations with strangers and service workers.

- Encourage older children to schedule their own appointments, make their own apologies, and solve their own issues (with a parent on deck to offer support, if needed).

- Suggest children--even young ones--place their own food order when dining out.

💜 **Planned "Privations"**

On occasion, plan activities which temporarily deprive children of their current standard of living in order to change perspective and develop appreciation (Harris, 2015).

- Practice healthier eating by doing a one day/week/month "no-sugar challenge," or give up eating unhealthy or fast food for a period of time.

- Camping is a great way to come to appreciate the  comforts of home and learn to do without certain luxuries. Inevitably, something is bound to be forgotten or go wrong, so problem-solving, substitution, or do-without strategies come into play, all of which teach resilience.

- More athletic types can venture on backpacking trips, run a 5K/10K (or even work up to a marathon). Families with older children can participate in challenging events like IronMan,

Spartan or Tough Mudder competitions, which have "lite" versions for beginners. Doing physically challenging activities spills over into emotional confidence as a child discovers, "I can do hard things."

- With older children, consider serving meals at a homeless shelter on a holiday when volunteers might be scarce. Along with learning to give without judging, seeing another's lack fosters gratitude for your own blessings.

- Consider a family volunteer vacation where your child will be giving back, while discovering the real day-to-day struggle for survival others in the world face.

- Another version of planned privation is financial education on budgeting and saving. Teaching a child to delay gratification by giving up what you want now in order to achieve or have something better later, reaps dividends in more than just financial security.

♥ **Laugh Often**

Find comedians, TV shows and movies that offer witty insights into the lighter side of life, and supply quotable quips the whole family can enjoy for years to come. *Beware sarcasm (with hostility disguised as humor) and outlaw put-downs in your home. Sayings like, "Way to go, Einstein" don't make anyone feel like a genius.* Wholesome shared laughter forges bonds between family members and provides an excellent stress buster.

♥ **Earned Achievements**

Develop a child's talents and interests; look for activities where *achievement is earned over time,* such as:

- Learning to play an instrument, participating in an orchestra or marching band, or singing in a choir.
- Participating in "non-glory" sports: swimming, wrestling, track/cross country, gymnastics or tennis.
- Developing skills in debate, speech, science, math, writing, art or photography.

♥ **Spiritual Foundations**

Share your belief in God (or a higher power) with your child. While there are multiple religions and paths to express spirituality, research shows a belief in something greater than yourself results in better health, less depression, greater empathy, more positive feelings (such as optimism and generosity), and less stress - even during difficult times.

> *"When we pray, we don't change the world, we change ourselves. We change our consciousness. We move from an individual, isolated making-things-happen kind of consciousness to a connection on the deepest level with the largest possible reality. When we pray, we stop trying to control life and remember that we belong to life. It is an opportunity to experience humility and recognize grace."*
> – Dr. Rachel Naomi Remen,
>   *Kitchen Table Wisdom* (Remen, 1996)

♥ Family History

Collect, compile, and communicate pictures and stories of resilience from your own life and the lives of ancestors. Stories of wanting, having, losing and gaining can help a child develop connection, courage and confidence to combat their own challenges and find happiness despite hardships.

♥ Leave home

- Give children autonomy opportunities in controlled environments.
- Sending a child to scout, sports or youth camps and conferences, or a mini-stay with relatives can foster self-reliance skills.
- Learning to work through feelings of homesickness or worry develops the independence necessary for future "adulting."

♥ Express love – everyday!

While is seems obvious, a child needs to regularly hear the words, "I love you." Children need to know their worth, and lovability does not have to be earned. Make it a habit to consistently communicate unconditional love. Consider using other loving and encouraging phrases, such as:

- I'm proud of *you* (not just what you've done)
- I believe in you
- You've got this
- Please forgive me (for times *you* are wrong)
- I'm here for you   (Wong, 2014)

Many of these practices overlap:

- Teach hard work and perseverance through play. Our family enjoys sandcastle building – with five-gallon buckets! This requires loading and lugging huge amounts of sand over a matter of hours. Even so, the satisfaction of creating photo-  worthy castles makes the effort worthwhile.

- "Fun Runs" and "5Ks-For-a-Cause" teach social and physical skills.

- Confident communication and employment go together. As teens, our sons went door-to-door promoting their lawn care business. Our daughter sold farm-fresh eggs to neighbors and snack bar items from a cooler at her brothers' sports games.

- Increased face time (and, therefore, decreased screen time) translates into more time for physical activities, play dates, learning and service.

- Family vacations can be a mix of work, play, and planned privation. Some families let their children earn "Disney Dollars" through extra chores before a trip to Disneyland. Travel provides a great chance to expose children to other cultures, foods, and ways of life. In addition, adventure activities like whitewater rafting, zip-lining and snorkeling offer opportunities to face and overcome fears in a relatively controlled setting.

The sooner we offer a child the opportunity for independence, communication, and pushing through hard things, the greater the reservoir of resilience available for future challenges.

It can be difficult or overwhelming to know where and how to begin helping a child to develop habits of success, especially when dealing with emotional matters. Below are 3 ways we can help our child chart a course to becoming his or her best self.

1) **Set objectives**. Teach a child to vividly picture in the mind and then write down a plan to achieve goals. Dr Gail Matthews, a psychology professor at the Dominican University in California, found, "that you become 42% more likely to achieve your goals and dreams, simply by writing them down on a regular basis." Sharing a written goal with someone (a partner in believing), increases the likelihood of succeeding (Morrissey, 2016). Encourage baby steps to get started, since once in motion, bodies tend to stay in motion.

2) **Teach accountability**. Pearson's Law states, "When performance is measured, performance improves. When performance is measured and reported back, the rate of improvement accelerates."
Identify specific, *behavioral* goals such as, "practice 20 minutes each day," or "finish chores and homework by 5 PM." Using measurable milestones allows you, and your child, to monitor progress, make modifications, and celebrate success.

3) **Encourage Growth**. Ditch perfectionism. Instead, offer opportunities for growth while simultaneously fostering emotional resilience with validation, should things go awry. Struggle is simply part of striving to be better at something, and challenges are welcomed. This belief generates a lifelong love of learning, and promotes emotional resilience essential for accomplishment.

Stanford University psychologist, Carol Dweck, coined the concept of mindset in her book, *Mindset: The New Psychology of Success*. According to Dweck, a mindset is a belief people hold about themselves (Dweck, 2006).

With a **fixed mindset**, children believe their basic qualities, whether smart or dumb, athletic or weak, etc., are fixed from birth, and talent alone creates success. Dweck's research suggests that children with this mindset believe there is no way to change, adapt, or grow. Instead of seeking to develop their minds or talents when they experience failure, they tell themselves they can't - or won't - be able to learn and improve. Sometimes, they make excuses and rationalize failure. A child may be unaware of this fixed mindset, which profoundly affects academic achievement, skill development, and interpersonal relationships.

Children with a **growth mindset** believe that brains and talent are simply a starting point, and most basic abilities can be developed through dedication and perseverance. Unafraid of failure or effort, a child with this mindset believes they can become smarter and/or stronger as they seek to learn more and work harder.

Most motivation comes from honoring difficulties, putting challenges in perspective, pushing ahead with perseverance, and tapping into reservoirs of resilience.

Recognizing that stressful experiences cultivate toughness to better tolerate and adapt to future challenges in life, we can offer encouragement to a child before, during or after a stressful situation. When weathering an upsetting incident or traumatic event, we can reassure that our child will, in fact, survive and can even thrive.

Extending validation through emotional first aid, helps a child become less likely to fear stress or change, and instead gain important life skills such as empathy, patience, or confidence. As a parent, our validation creates a framework of emotional support, helping our child develop the ability to overcome challenges they will surely encounter in life.

Emotional validation from a parent acts like a trellis which offers support to a growing plant.

Remember, the trellis is simply steady and constant while the plant inches up, *on its own*, climbing to reach its full potential. Making our child's social, physical, emotional, and spiritual nurturing a priority will develop the hardiness and resilience necessary to achieve his or her greatest growth.

Chapter 12: The Body Doesn't Lie

*"Pain isn't the truth; it's what you have
to get through in order to find the truth."*
- Deepak Chopra

Pain is the body's way of alerting you to danger or alarm. If you're touching a hot surface with your hand, the brain sends a message of pain to promptly remove your palm. Likewise, should you sprain your ankle the brain will activate a pain signal to get you to stop walking on that foot.

Yet, we often feel symptoms of pain without being able to identify the cause. You wake up with a stiff neck or find yourself coughing when you don't feel sick.

A child coping with continuous or unaddressed emotional distress will often manifest physical issues.

Baily was a fourteen-year-old bed-wetter. Potty-trained at three, she suddenly regressed at age six. For eight years, she had been unable to stay dry at night, limiting her ability to have sleepovers or attend overnight girls' camps.

During her session, we looked at what was going in her life at age six. Two major events took place: the family moved to a different city, and her dad was in a serious car accident. Both incidents left her feeling out of control and unsafe.

The family moved several more times over the years, so Baily was constantly in new situations and feeling the loss of friends. Repeatedly experiencing unexpected changes caused feelings of apprehensiveness, dread, and insecurity. Currently feeling overwhelmed with school, cross-country, and drivers' education classes, she reported feeling like she "just couldn't hold the pressure in anymore."

Once we validated those early events and current feelings, Baily's body felt safe and ready to manage the pressures of life. From that time forward, she has been able to stay dry all night.

 **Like a red warning light flashing on a car dashboard, symptoms of illness or pain may indicate feelings which need attention.**

Often, instead of identifying emotions, human nature causes us to resist, suppress, or ignore the things that don't feel good. Fearing pain, it's natural to push away, push down, or push aside any potentially negative feelings. Like a little child playing peek-a-boo, we cover our eyes  believing the rest of the world will suddenly disappear.

Feelings, however, don't play that way. While daily hurts usually fade, traumatic incidents--and the feelings or beliefs generated because of them--can burrow into the cells, tissues, and organs of the body. Unprocessed feelings lock into receptor sites in the brain; they create energetic cysts that block our body's natural rhythm, flow, and healing.

Suppressed emotions must be allowed to surface.

Like the tremendous energy it takes to hold a beach ball under water, feelings can *temporarily* be held down. Eventually, untreated feelings have to go somewhere; either **exploding outward** (in angry outbursts of heated words or acts of physical aggression), or **imploding inward** (leaving the body vulnerable to emotional

or physical symptoms where the body cries out for attention).

Physical symptoms may signal
unresolved emotional pain.

The body doesn't lie.

Even when our child can't identify or express situations or people creating distress, the body has no access to denial. Emotions of fear, anger, humiliation, embarrassment, guilt or shame all generate physical responses in the body.

Anxiety or panic attacks can include genuine physical distress such as accelerated heart rate, dizziness, chest pain, trembling, numbness, chills or hot flashes and shortness of breath. Panic attacks typically rise suddenly and can feel overwhelming. Anxiety attacks are generally gradual and related to anticipation of a stressful event or situation. Both types of attacks are caused by a fear-based reaction to thoughts or beliefs (whether true or not) in the mind.

We can encourage our child to listen for messages from the body to help identify feelings.

As we observe signs of physical distress, we can suggest a child notice the way his or her body is reacting. Signals of irregular breathing, flushed skin, tense muscles, averted eyes, or stomach cramps are cues to the body has a message that needs to be heard and validated.

She might detect clammy hands, "butterflies" in the stomach, or a burning throat. He might notice buzzing ears, or jumpy legs, or a heavy chest. Each sensation is a clue to possible stuck emotions.

The body is metaphorical, so the location of physical symptoms provides clues to emotional needs the body may be trying to communicate. Skin issues, such as rashes or eczema, can show irritation or sensitivity to something in a child's environment. Constipation corresponds to something which can't be let go. Earaches can represent things you don't want to hear, and sore throats signify things you can't say. Shoulder pain can represent burdens. Back pain symbolizes feeling a lack of support or financial worry. Hips, legs, or feet represent an inability to move forward. Bladder issues often embody being "pissed-off," and bed-wetting may stem from unresolved hurt or anger.

For a list of body and emotional messages by symptoms, see Resources, pages 258-266.

The belly is often a barometer of a child's emotional states and stresses, with physical problems such as: diarrhea, ulcers, irritable bowel syndrome, heartburn, and upset stomach. Listen for words such as, "My tummy doesn't feel good," or, "It feels like I have a knot in my stomach."

Studies now show that 95% of the body's serotonin (involved in mood control, depression, and suppressing aggression) is actually found *within our intestines*, not our brain. In a sense, we have *two brains;* the thinking one inside our head, and the feeling one inside our gut (Hadhazy, 2010).

In addition, 50% of the body's neurons are found in the gut, and offer a deeply instinctual way of communicating with the brain and central nervous system. This means we have to pay attention not only to conscious thoughts and feelings, but also body symptoms and signals.

161

When it comes to safeguarding a child from sexual abuse, protection starts by teaching a child to listen to the wisdom of the brain and the gut.

Teach a child to trust feelings and sensations felt in the body designed to warn them of danger. Sadly, a menace is often found in the palm of a child's hand. Officer David Gomez of the Meridian Idaho Police Department suggests that many parents have no idea what their child is doing on devices that connect to the internet.

More likely pressured by peers than predators, Gomez reports the rampant perils of "sexting" by teens: "By about tenth grade, 70 percent of the girls at high schools have sent out their naked pictures. We have 10th, 11th, 12th graders who are trying to get nude photos of their classmates and they extort them to either get the pictures or get money or get iTunes cards. But it's already a very common thing that they know they can extort their female classmates for naked pictures. We have adult men predators who pretend to be girls to get the naked pictures of the boys and extort them as well" (Fields, 2017).

Sexual abuse statistics are staggering: 67% of victims of sexual assault are under 18. We often think that the danger is "out there". In fact, more than 90% of child sexual abuse victims know their attacker (Snyder, 2000). Children living in homes with parental discord, divorce or domestic violence show a higher risk of being sexually abused.

Kallie was physically and sexually abused, from the age of ten, by her older brother. Her divorced mother would leave the two kids home alone while she went out partying with friends. When Kallie finally got the courage to tell her mother what was happening, her mother replied, "Did you enjoy it?" Unfortunately, this response left Kallie feeling like the abuse was her fault.

According to the Child Sex Abuse Prevention and Protection Center, "There is NO sex offender profile. Abusers can be anyone: family members, neighbors, friends, doctors, coaches, youth leaders or clergy members. Many times, these 'respected' abusers remain undetected."

If you think it's wrong, you're right.

Children must be taught how to reduce risks, and recognize danger signals sent as feelings in the body. For example, we want to teach that an unsafe touch makes us feel confused, scared, uncomfortable, or icky. Safe touches make us feel safe, happy, and loved. The same sensations occur when a child is told to keep an unsafe secret versus a safe secret.

Advice from www.safersmarterteens.org counsels, "Encourage your child to tell you or a trusted adult about any touch that makes them feel unsafe, and to keep telling until they are heard and helped. Children who feel they can talk to a parent, caregiver or trusted adult about anything are less susceptible to being victimized."

Should a child divulge abuse, whether from unsafe touch, internet solicitations, or unsafe secrets, validate what happened and verify what has been disclosed. Don't make a child feel like it's their fault or they are in trouble. Instead, gather evidence, block platforms or people on the internet and if necessary contact the police.

Lauren Book, a victim of sexual abuse as a child, has created a *free* family curriculum with questions, tips and plans to prevent abuse through education and awareness. Lauren states, "We teach our kids to 'stop, drop and roll' if there's a fire, and what to do in the event of a natural disaster, but children are far more likely to be victims of sexual abuse than a fire-related emergency." This tremendous resource to help families prevent abuse and protect childhood can be found at www.laurenskids.org.

Taking time to prepare and prevent potential issues before they happen is our best protection. We must help our child recognize and respond to the valuable signals the body sends.

Remember, all pain has a message of some kind.

Whether relating to a physical condition or psychological situation, trust that pain is the body's way of sending an urgent signal. The key is to decode the meaning behind the symptom and treat the root cause.

We must be responsive to risk factors that may trigger pain or distress in a child. Social situations, experiencing or witnessing trauma, having another mental health disorder or experiencing a stressful life event such as family conflict or parental divorce can have an impact on the body.

For lesser hurts, validation may be all that's needed. For greater pain, see the treating trauma tools taught the "Repair" section of this book.

Part III: REPAIR

Treating Trauma and Emotional Drama

Chapter 13: Taming the Tiger

"The cat ignored becomes the tiger."
– Carl Jung

Validation is a powerful first aid tool for healing everyday emotional bumps and bruises. But how do we handle a child's extremely traumatic experiences, severe emotional shocks, or debilitating medical diagnoses? We look for the inciting event.

We often think trauma has to be caused by a big event. The truth is the brain doesn't differentiate between big or small trauma. They both trigger the same survival reaction in the brain.

Imagine a traumatic incident like getting a deeply-embedded splinter.

To get to a favorite beach in California, we had to cross a small bridge made of railroad ties. While walking barefoot across this bridge, my sister's friend, Brittany, suddenly howled and hopped in pain with blood dripping from her foot. Once seated, we easily identified a wooden splinter wedged in her big toe. Removing the splinter, cleaning the wound, and wrapping her foot, we helped her hobble home, assuming we had resolved the problem.

Weeks later, Brittany's toe, still throbbing with pain, prompted her parents to seek a specialist. Upon closer examination, the doctor discovered a sliver of that splinter so deeply embedded and festering with infection, that surgery was required to drain the abscess. Once removed, her body was finally able to heal.

Emotional injuries require a parallel practice. Just like a physical splinter, a troubling incident must be assessed, addressed, and remedied for healing to happen. In most cases, the hurt is hard to ignore, requiring immediate attention. When overlooked, a wound is more likely to worsen.

Typically, the most potentially wounding situations involve pain caused in familial relationships. Circumstances of

 divorce, estrangement and abuse can affect a child's sense of worth and safety. Any of these events can alter a child's reference point for love, creating a broken belief that love = abandonment, betrayal, and hurt.

Children who have experienced emotional, physical or sexual abuse assess the trauma based on their perspective of how they felt, and the culpability of the offender. Interestingly, children often feel more victimized by a non-offending parent who they judge failed to protect them.

Adoption is another arena which may imbed deep distress inside a child. In her book, *The Primal Wound*, Nancy Newton Verrier suggests the severing of the bond between an adopted child and the birthmother, "affects the adoptee's sense of Self and often manifests in a sense of loss, basic mistrust, anxiety, depression, emotional and/or behavioral problems and difficulties in relationships with significant others" (Verrier, 1993). The emotional impact is experienced in various ways by each party in the adoption triad – the child, the birthmother, and the adoptive parents.

Everyday life is potentially wounding, depending on the meaning a child's mind places on what is experienced.

 Carl Jung, founder of analytical psychiatry, suggested, "The cat ignored becomes the tiger." When my daughter experienced the trauma of being left behind, I had no idea she required more than to be told I was sorry she had been forgotten.

Unaware of the need to delve deeper to resolve the fear triggered by this traumatic experience, Katie's unnamed beliefs and unacknowledged emotions were pushed below the surface to fester. In her case, the unprocessed trauma wasn't evident for five years, until triggered  by a related incident. By then, the cat had become a roaring tiger that needed to be tamed.

Kids today are reporting more feelings of isolation, worry, sadness, sensitivity, entitlement, being misunderstood, and general dissatisfaction than ever before (Nott, 2013). Moreover, the teen brain is extremely sensitive to stress and the pressure to perform. Yet, instead of looking at the symptoms, we should be looking for the inciting event.

Truly, any distressing incident, when left untreated, can fester into anxiety, panic attacks, depression, social phobias,

171

separation anxiety, behavior problems and even suicide. In contrast, pressure and pain are relieved when a child receives care to repair emotional injuries, allowing the body's natural wisdom to complete the healing process.

In order to truly help someone hurting, the "negative" has to be cleared out, making space for the "positive."

Whether seeking to quickly remove an emotional "splinter" before it festers, or treat suppressed hurts which may generate physical or psychological symptoms, apply the following 3 steps.

The Emotional 911 Sequence:

1) Reveal: Name and Tame

Identify or name the feeling as it surfaces

2) Release: Feel and Deal

Let go of unwanted feelings using validation and visualization

3) Replace: Choose and Infuse

Name and claim a better feeling, thought, or belief

You can imagine these three steps like a bridge over turbulent rapids, offering safe passage to the other side without the danger of being swept away.

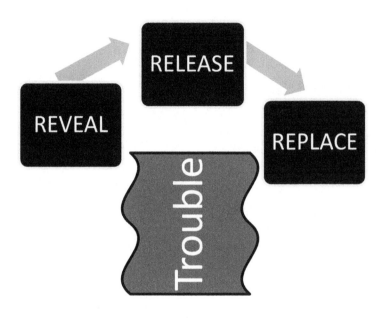

As first responders, parents must be prepared with Emotional 911 skills to help children identify the wound, instead of becoming the wound.

Applying this 3-step Emotional 911 sequence allows us to help our child address and process troubling situations. As emotional wounds are revealed and healed, we guide our child to find a more hopeful future on the other side of whatever he or she is experiencing.

Chapter 14: Name and Tame

*"If we don't know what we feel,
we don't know what we need."*
- Milan & Kay Yerkovich

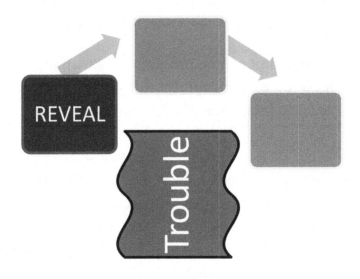

**The ability to identify exactly what we are
feeling allows us to do something about it.**

Identify or name the feeling as it surfaces:

Reveal means, *"to make something visible that had been hidden or covered."* Emotional health requires the ability to accurately identify the emotional cues of others, as well as our own.

Can you imagine going to the doctor with an injury, and simply stating there is something wrong somewhere in your body? No. You would want to describe when and how the pain started, along with the precise location and intensity of the pain. This way, the doctor could assess the problem at a detailed level and determine care *specific* to your needs.

Similarly, with emotional pain we need an accurate, detailed account of what our child is feeling to determine exactly what he or she needs. No matter the cause, how a child feels and reacts is what creates the pain or distress.

Remember, the problem is not what happened or is currently happening; it is how a child feels because of what happened.

In *Writing as a Way of Healing*, Louise DeSalvo explains, "We receive a shock or a blow or experience trauma in our lives. In exploring it, examining it and putting it into words, we stop seeing it as a random unexplained event. We can begin to understand the order behind appearances. Expressing it in language robs the event of its power to hurt us; it also assuages our pain" (DeSalvo, 1999).

Awareness is the first step in relieving distressing emotions.

One of the most important skills a child can be taught in the early years involves emotional awareness. Discerning

differences among emotional states such as sadness, frustration, fear, anger, and happiness requires a broader vocabulary of feeling words. The capacity to recognize what one is feeling in any given situation is the gateway to emotional resilience.

Children younger than five years old tend to show their feelings through behavior, because they don't yet have the emotional vocabulary to express their feelings. Often, parents react to annoying behavior (like whining or fussing) with irritation rather than trying to understand what a child wishes to communicate.

Emotional Literacy

Most children, and even many adults, tend to identify feelings with a limited emotional vocabulary, consisting of a handful of emotions: good/bad, happy/sad, fine/mad, stressed, and tired. Incomplete emotional language restricts the ability to pinpoint true feelings.

Emotional literacy is the ability to:

1) Understand, manage, and express emotions productively

2) Listen and empathize with the emotions of others

3) Repair emotional problems

To be emotionally literate is to be able to handle emotions in a way that improves your personal power, and improves the quality of life around you. Emotional literacy improves relationships, creates loving possibilities between people, makes co-operative work possible, and facilitates the feeling of community (Steiner, 1997).

Teaching children to be descriptive in *naming* emotions as a framework for how they feel, *without claiming* that feeling as who they are, is crucial for resilience.

Ideally, our child will say, "I *feel* unhappy" versus, "I *am* unhappy." The first statement acknowledges a passing feeling, while the other can become part of a child's identity.

Moreover, training a child to *name, but not blame* others for his or her emotional response, is essential for accountability. Our child might notice *feeling* mad or sad as a knee-jerk reaction to an incident, but no one can *make* you mad or sad. Our reaction and response is our responsibility.

When a child says he or she *is* stressed, it usually signals a bunch of feelings piled up on top of each other.

Imagine distressing emotions like blocks stacked one on top of another. With the intent to topple the tower, you can either pull off blocks one by one, or simply pull the underpinning blocks, and everything above tumbles down.

Start by applying the Hero Validation Recipe to encourage discussion and identify pain points. This is where asking the question, "What's the worst part?" allows us to focus on the foundational feelings causing pain or discomfort.

We can encourage our child to use emotional vocabulary words by asking, "How does this situation make you feel?" Most likely, upsetting circumstances will create a combination of several feelings, not just one perfect word. We can follow up by asking, "Anything else?" or, "Is there more?"

Next, we can invite a child to put his or her hand over the part of the body where he or she feels discomfort, and ask, "What else do I feel?" or, "What do I need to feel better?" Just by acknowledging the body's message of discomfort, a child will often feel some relief.

The goal is to help our child notice and name feelings in any situation or setting.

Just like learning any new skill, growing an emotional vocabulary takes time and practice. We can expand our child's emotional literacy by teaching feeling words and definitions during everyday conversations and play, as well as through intentional activities.

Below are ways we can help our child notice the nuances of emotions, and facilitate adding feeling words and definitions to a child's vocabulary.

Mealtimes: Eating meals together provides a built-in opportunity to have feeling discussions. In our home, each family member gets a chance to tell their low and high experience of the day. We encourage each child to start with the low or less pleasant occurrence, and end with something good. In each case, we make sure the person is encouraged to express *how they feel* about what happened, so it can be validated or celebrated.

It's important to focus on things that make us feel good. When a child knows he or she will need to report on a happy event each day, the brain is trained to look for, and accentuate, the positive.

For Younger Children

As our child experiences different affected states, we can expand his or her emotional vocabulary by providing feeling names and definitions. For example, when a toddler smiles, we could say, "There's my happy girl." When a child shows reluctance to get moving, we might ask, "Why are you *acting* so grumpy?" (Notice we don't ask, "Why are *you* so grumpy?" in order to separate behavior from identity.)

Questions can help our child develop emotional awareness and self-reflection skills. As we demonstrate naming emotions, we allow our child to begin to identify them on their own.

Feeling Faces:

We can expand vocabulary by pairing a picture of a "feeling face" with the appropriate emotional label. Preschoolers seem to be better at recognizing feelings from drawn pictures first, and then progressing to photographs.

In preparing a "feeling faces" resource for this book, I enlisted the help of Aubree, my seven-year-old neighbor. Using a list of emotions provided for Aubree to draw, her mother, Lana, found that she had to define some of the unfamiliar feeling words to Aubree.

By giving examples of situations where certain feelings might arise, or by making a face herself to show how a certain emotion might look, Lana taught Aubree several new emotional vocabulary words in the process.

Use the Feeling Faces Grid, illustrated by Aubree Hope, found in the Resources section on page 255. Better yet, help your child to create his or her own drawings of feeling faces.

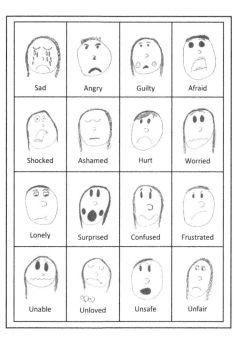

Mood Meter:

Younger children can be encouraged to "check-in" each morning by selecting a feeling face picture from a chart on the refrigerator, and marking it with a magnet. A child can be encouraged to notice how his or her feelings change throughout the day by naming the feeling, and moving the magnet to new feeling face.

Books:

Children's books are an excellent way to introduce children to feelings. Books written specifically about emotions contain numerous feeling words which may be new to our child.

When reading books, we can stop at any point in the story and ask what our child thinks the main character might be feeling, or how our child feels about what is happening in the story.

We can help our child notice how a character might show emotions using body language or facial expressions. This might be eyes widening in surprise, nail biting for nervousness, or looking down when ashamed.

Children's Books featuring Feeling Faces and Words:

• *The Way I Feel* by Janan Cain • *Emotions in Motion* by Rose Stanley, Lisa Allen (Illustrator) • *The Feelings Book* by Todd Parr • *On Monday When It Rained* by Cherryl Kachenmeister, • *Glad Monster, Sad Monster: A Book About Feelings* by Anne Miranda, Ed Emberley (Illustrator) • *My Many Colored Days* by Dr. Seuss, Steve Johnson (Illustrator), Lou Fancher (Illustrator) • *When Sophie Gets Angry--Really, Really Angry* by Molly Bang • *Feelings* (Reading Rainbow Book) by Aliki • *I'm Mad (Dealing With Feelings)* by Elizabeth Crary, Jean Whitney (Illustrator) • *I'm Frustrated (Dealing With Feelings)* by Elizabeth Crary, Jean Whitney (Illustrator) • *When I Feel Angry* by Cornelia Maude Spelman, Nancy Cote (Illustrator)

These same questions could be asked while viewing television shows or movies, whether we pause during the program, or discuss it together afterwards. Asking our child to identify the character's emotions, or their own feelings as the viewer, allows our child to experience new and unfamiliar feelings.

Mirrors: Give a child a small, hand-held mirror. As you read a storybook, when a character expresses emotion, invite your child to make the corresponding faces while looking at him or herself in the mirror.

More Feeling Activities:

Action Poems or Songs: Seek out songs or rhymes that help a child recognize feelings. For example:

> **If You Chance to Meet A Frown**
> If you chance to meet a frown,
> Do not let it stay.
> Quickly turn it upside-down,
> And smile that frown away.
> No one likes a frowning face.
> Change it for a smile.
> Make the world a better place,
> By smiling all the while.
> *Words: Daniel Taylor, Music: Anon.*

I Spy: Put feeling face pictures up around the house. Give your child a magnifying glass, and allow him or her to hunt for pictures or drawings of faces showing different emotions. When anyone finds a picture, he or she calls out, "I spy!" Together, you can label the face and think of a time one of you felt that feeling. Another idea is to invent a story telling what might have happened to motivate the person pictured to exhibit that feeling.

Games: Look for games which help children identify feelings in themselves or others. Classic board games like *LIFE, SORRY* or *Chutes and Ladders* allow children to experience emotional reactions from setbacks or successes.

For feeling-specific games, consider:

- **Feeling Dice:** Create your own "Feeling-Dice" game by covering each side of small milk cartons or boxes with a different feeling face. To play: Take turns tossing the dice, labeling the emotion on the face and/or describing a time one of you felt that way.

- **Feeling BINGO:** Make/use a "Feeling Faces BINGO Board." Invite your child to cross out the faces on the board as you read a book or watch a movie. Or, take turns choosing a square from each of your boards to try and get five in a row.

  For more fun, choose a square by making a feeling face to indicate the intended selection, and see if the other player(s) can identify the emotion.

- **Friends and Neighbors--The Helping Game** by Peaceable Kingdom. In playing this game and reading about the feelings and needs of the characters, parents can help their children recognize feelings in others. This is the first step to building empathy. Ages three and up.

- **Feelings and Dealings** (available online): This game, designed for kids aged 3-6 years, with 48 expressive cards and 24 common emotions, provides 8 games designed to develop emotional fluency and empathy through fun and engaging play.
  https://gameonfamily.com/feelingsanddealings/

- **Game of Mixed Emotions** (available online): This card game teaches kids that emotions are temporary, and it's okay to feel a variety of feelings. Features 24 different emotions with each of the 12 characters in the game displaying 4 categories of emotions (based on the Yale Center for Emotional Intelligence). These categories are identified by color and energy type:
  - *Red Fire: High Energy;* uncomfortable emotions like Mad, Scared, Embarrassed, Hungry, Worried, and Frustrated
  - *Blue Clouds: Low Energy;* uncomfortable emotions like Sad, Hurt, Tired, Sick, Shy, and Distracted
  - *Green Clovers: Low Energy;* comfortable emotions like Calm, Patient, Kind, Safe, Peaceful, and Grateful
  - *Yellow Suns: High Energy;* comfortable emotions like Joy, Happy, Helpful, Excited, Proud, and Brave

  https://www.kickstarter.com/projects/1084962886/the-game-of-mixed-emotions-teaching-emotional-voca

For Older Children

FEELINGS GRID: All emotions are not equal. There is a vast difference between feeling scared and afraid, sad and hurt, or disappointed and rejected. Many children miss the subtle shades of feelings because they do not have exposure to terms and definitions for them.

Once a child can read, using a word bank with a list of familiar or new emotional vocabulary words may prompt more precise descriptions of what is being felt.

A	B	C	D
Abandoned	Annoyed	Avoidance	Anxious
Abused	Bad	Awful	Hurt
Alone	Bitter	Blame	Intimidated
Cheated	Blocked	Defensive	Lost
Confused	Critical	Disgust	Overwhelmed
Depressed	Disappointed	Distrust	Panic
Frustrated	Discouraged	Doubtful	Scared
Heartbroken	Dumb	Dread	Stuck
Helpless	Embarrassed	Forgetful	Surprised
Hesitant	Failure	Indecisive	Terrified
Hopeless	Forced	Inferior	Threatened
Homesick	Forgetful	Insecurity	Trapped
Humiliated	Hatred	Irresponsible	Unprotected
Insecure	Ignored	Judgmental	Unsupported
Left Out	Jealous	Naughty	Unsuccessful
Lonely	Resentful	Not enough	Unworthy
Nervous	Restricted	Responsible	Unsafe
Shy	Rejected	Self-rejected	Unloved
Tired	Shocked	Shame	Unloveable
Ugly	Surprised	Stubborn	Unwanted
Unhappy	Stifled	Stupid	Violated
Uncomfortable	Rushed	Powerless	Vulnerable
Unnoticed	Unappreciated	Unable	Weak
Worried	Unfair	Unimportant	Worthless

Feeling Faces and Feeling Words Grids, provided in the Resources section of this book, can help a child pinpoint what he or she is really feeling. This allows us to accurately acknowledge any painful feelings, and provide the relief needed.

Watching movies or television together: Instead of letting the kids just "veg" in front of the tube, look for TV programs and movies which provide opportunities to discuss challenges faced and overcome by the main character.

Encourage a child to identify emotions one or more characters in the show may have been feeling at various times. Consider brainstorming different ways a character could have responded to what happened, and how good or bad choices affected the outcome of the story.

Evaluating the experiences of others can help a child develop empathy and problem-solving skills.

Suggested movies and TV shows that help develop empathy:

• *Shrek* • *Dumbo* • *Despicable Me* • *Finding Nemo* • *Antz*
• *Harry Potter* • *Bambi* • *Inside Out* • *Babe* • *Spiderman*
• *The Karate Kid* • *Rudy* • *Charlotte's Web* • *Cinderella*
• *Frozen* • *Zootopia* • *Freaky Friday* • *A Wrinkle in Time*

Find more empathy viewing lists using the links below:

https://www.commonsensemedia.org/lists/movies-that-inspire-empathy#

http://micheleborba.com/100-movies-for-kids-5-to-17-that-teach-9-crucial-empathy-habits/

https://www.tidbits-cami.com/the-top-10-tv-shows-for-kids-that-teach-good-things-on-netflix/

Mood Measuring Phone App: Smartphones can be used for identifying, naming, and shifting emotions. The Yale Center for Emotional Intelligence has an insightful Smartphone application called, "The Mood Meter."

This app allows a user to regularly check-in with feelings throughout the day, expand emotional vocabulary, notice patterns of feelings over time, and learn effective strategies to regulate and manage feelings.

One of my favorite parts is the opportunity to acknowledge what you are feeling right now, then swipe to select a better feeling to shift your mood.

Note: Current cost is $0.99. Don't be fooled by some free apps which supposedly "read" your mood for you using a finger scan on your phone touch pad.

**Learning to label what is being felt
without judgment, allows a child to feel
and deal with uncomfortable emotions.**

Identify or name the unwanted emotion

A) Recognize signals – whether physical pain or emotional distress.

B) Initiate the Validation Hero Recipe, inviting story and self-reflection, to determine what a child needs to W-I-N.

C) Encourage a child to use emotional vocabulary words or feeling faces to identify uncomfortable emotions and/or broken beliefs involved.

Remember, it's not what has happened or is happening, but how our child feels about it that matters.

Naming is taming. Giving our child words to feel and deal with negative experiences allows distressing emotions, along with any harmful beliefs, to be revealed and then released. This provides the heart and mind space needed to replace with better feelings and beliefs so our child can employ and enjoy a full spectrum of positive emotions.

Chapter 15: Feel and Deal

*"Sometimes you don't realize the weight
of what you've been carrying until you
feel the relief of its release."*
- Unknown

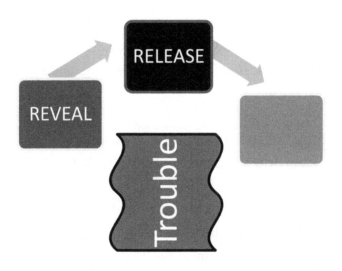

**Let go of unwanted feelings using
validation and visualization.**

Once we help our child develop an awareness of feelings, along with a vocabulary to accurately reveal them, we can teach him or her how to release unwanted feelings.

Many parents teach children to *MANAGE* feelings with self-regulation strategies, such as:

- taking a break when bothered
- breathing deeply when distressed

- speaking up when sad
- moving the body when mad

or, problem-solving solutions:

- pro/con lists
- brainstorming solutions
- conflict resolution
- interventions

These methods are useful in *coping* with everyday emotional bumps and bruises. However, in times of greater crisis or trauma, *clearing* unhelpful feelings and/or unhealthy beliefs is crucial.

Under stress, the body's survival instincts can override the brain's ability to think clearly.

For my daughter, Katie, fearing that once she left the house she could be forgotten triggered the body's flight/fight/freeze response. Her belief kept the threat of this unlikely occurrence in the forefront of her mind.

Short-circuiting her brain's ability to consider options and trust that she was capable of handling a similar situation should it happen again, the chemical spill of stress hormones left her in a constant state of anxiety.

When something stressful happens, the body has three common responses: fight, flight, or freeze.

The fight-or-flight response triggers the body's subconscious method for survival, creating chemical spills of adrenaline and cortisol. As a result, our bodies tense up, speed up, and prepare for action just as if we were being chased by a lion. The brain becomes focused on getting away from--or fighting off--the threat.

The freeze response is believed to occur if neither fight nor flight is an option. When overwhelmed, overpowered, or trapped, humans respond as many animals do and play dead.

> *"When the discharge of trauma energy is interrupted and incomplete, the excess adrenaline is still surging around the body, trying to do what it is designed to do: provide energy for a fight, flight, or freeze response.*
>
> *When the frontal brain overrides the hindbrain, and demands that the body stop trembling and shaking, the body has to do something to contain the adrenaline energy. It "freezes" it into body tissues with chemical bonds to hold it still.*
>
> *This frozen adrenaline energy remains locked in the muscles and fascia and organs and nervous system until it can be discharged; sometimes for the rest of a person's life. This "held" energy can create a multitude of symptoms and compensating behaviors"* (Sea, Somatic Trauma Release).

Not necessarily a conscious choice, the primitive brain takes over to protect us from greater psychological harm. By shutting down our attention systems in the moment, this survival instinct temporarily shields us from trauma.

Ultimately, a traumatic incident will require validation and resolution; otherwise, the upset may cause physical or psychological symptoms to manifest.

Since there is nothing we can do about the body's innate survival reflex, the only thing we can control is our response to incited feelings.

When something stressful happens, the <u>mind</u> has three common responses: blow-up, push down, or pass through.

BLOW-UP:

While someone is hurt or hurting, anger is often used as a smoke screen to either mask painful feelings, or to allow the

 person to appear stronger than he or she really feels. I call this, "The Pufferfish Effect." When feeling threatened, a puffer fish blows-up, pushing its spikes out as a way to seem larger in order to protect itself from danger or attack.

People do the same thing. Feeling hurt, shamed, or unworthy, some children will blow-up, using anger to hide pain. Unfortunately, the anger gets expressed while true hurt feelings stay stuck inside.

As a new school year was ready to start, sixth-grader, Steve, had told his mom, "I can't wait to go to Middle School where kids there won't know me as 'the angry kid.'" Yet, the first day of school, when Steve was unable to correctly enter a computer password during keyboarding class, he lost his cool with his teacher and himself. Steve's mom noticed this pattern of anger any time Steve struggled to understand directions or attempt new things.

In our session, I asked Steve what anger felt like in his body. A superhero fan, Steve said when he felt angry his body felt like The Hulk, where he turned into somebody else, and it felt like his head wasn't connected to his body anymore. A perfect example of the "Puffer-Fish Effect," (where one needs to feel bigger and stronger),  *I helped Steve recognize and reveal the painful feelings hiding beneath his anger.*

Talking together, we identified a "pain point" where Steve felt he was constantly competing to keep up with his older brothers, especially when his next-oldest sibling would claim to be better at everything. The belief, "I can't keep up," caused Steve to feel stupid and inferior.

I invited Steve to close his eyes and imagine he could see the rage and hurt in his body, which he reported appeared "red." I then asked him to clench his fists and imagine collecting all of the "red" from his body into his hands. I asked him to pretend that those feelings were now contained in an object held in his hands that he could release. When I asked what object he imagined seeing, he replied, "Oobleck."

Unfamiliar with this word, I looked at Steve's mom  who explained that Oobleck is a slimy substance made from water and cornstarch. It acts like a liquid but becomes solid when force is applied to it. The energy put into gripping the substance is what keeps it firm, yet as soon as it's released, the solid ball melts into liquid. (Just like holding and releasing emotions in the body.)

Steve said that he was ready to release the anger and hurtful feelings he named, so I asked him to open his hands and imagine the Oobleck oozing through his fingers, until his palms were empty, and the feelings were drained.

I encouraged him to use this visualization anytime he felt frustration or anger in his body in the future. This would then make space to replace anger with a better feeling.

(Note: Just for fun, I am including the Oobleck recipe in the Resources section at the back of this book. Consider letting your child experiment with this goo to be familiar with the sensation of how "letting go" offers effortless release.)

Elizabeth Kubler-Ross, a Swiss-American psychologist, observed that a child's natural anger and emotional outbursts last about fifteen seconds. Shaming or blaming a child for *feeling* angry may block its natural release.

Left unexpressed, emotions may get stuck and become a form of self-pity that lingers for years. Kubler-Ross points out that people who weren't allowed a natural expression of anger in childhood will often, "marinate in self-pity as adults, and are difficult to be around" (Northrup, 2006).

PUSH DOWN:

Another common response is to stuff, repress, or push down negative feelings created by stress, conflict, worry, anxiety, or fear. Some will stuff emotions, turning to food or mind-numbing substances and actions, such as smoking pot or tuning out with video games. Others suppress painful emotions by becoming cold, withdrawn, or depressed.

Resembling pushing down trash in a can, these coping methods leave layers of unprocessed pain to build up in the cells, organs, and tissues of the body.

Seeking to suppress emotional pain is especially harmful, since feelings operate with an all-or-nothing valve.

Eventually, buried emotions may surface as headaches, stomach aches, or other physical or mental symptoms.

Moreover, trying to block sadness or pain often means a child is unable to experience happiness or love.

Children are regularly exposed to potentially stressful situations. It's not always *feeling* emotion that causes problems; sometimes, it is how the feelings are handled. Thus, as a parent, the way we react to a child's fear, anger, sadness, shame, or jealousy is critical.

Our response when a child expresses feelings determines whether emotional development progresses or gets derailed.

For example: Imagine a mom with her six-year-old son in the checkout line at the grocery store. Little Jimmy sees the rows of candy bars, gum, and toys, and points to the treats.

Mom shakes her head "no," and Jimmy begins to throw a tantrum, or to "blow-up."

At this point Mom could say, "Quit crying right now, you brat!" or, "Stop screaming or you're never getting a treat again!" As most of us have witnessed this type of battle in a store, we know that either command will probably escalate the emotional level without resolving the tantrum.

Instead, a healthy and validating response could be, "I see you really want a treat. They do look yummy. It's okay to feel disappointed that we aren't going to buy one today." At this point, Mom can offer an alternative solution such as, "Let's plan to make cookies at home this weekend," or, "After we eat lunch we can have a treat."

Reactive statements shown in the first two responses demand that Jimmy "push down" his feelings. In the third example, Jimmy's mom validates his desire and feelings, while reminding Jimmy he can choose to control his actions.

PASS THROUGH:

The healthiest response is to allow emotions to pass  through as they arise. Have you ever looked up at the clouds and seen a familiar shape? Perhaps one cloud looked like a rabbit, a butterfly, or a heart, and you pointed out the figure to another person, asking if they could see it, too. However, within minutes, the cloud shape would shift, and the image would collapse.

Similarly, we can encourage a child to feel and deal with distressing emotions by noticing and naming negative feelings, and then letting them naturally pass through like clouds moving through the sky.

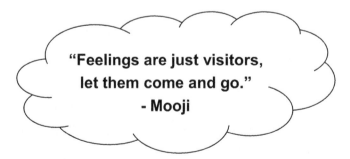

"Feelings are just visitors,
let them come and go."
- Mooji

Flipping Carl Jung's insight, we can train a child that "the tiger ignored becomes the cat," as we validate an ambushing thought into an agreeable kitten.

With my daughter, the placebo "Thinking Pill" provided a pause for her to choose a different response to upsetting thoughts, and push through apprehensive situations. Over time, the ability to feel the fear and know it would be fleeting allowed her "tiger" to be tamed.

By receiving validation for whatever feeling surfaces, and trusting that emotion will quickly pass, our child can release unwanted feelings and reach for a better feeling instead.

The goal is to quickly identify and release unwanted feelings.

Stories are told of hunters in Africa and India capturing monkeys. Using a hollowed-out coconut chained to a stake, the coconut has a treat of banana or rice inside which can be grabbed through a small hole. A monkey's hand fits through the hole, but once he clenches his fist, it is too big to back out of the hole.

The monkey is only trapped because he refuses to release what he's holding. If the monkey would simply let go of the treat, he could easily pull out his hand and be free.

Similarly, we want our children to avoid holding onto unwanted feelings and becoming trapped in negativity. Think of it like this: If our child picked up a snake, how long would we want him or her to hold onto it? Our urgent desire would be for our child to release the snake before it can cause lasting harm.

Science shows negative thoughts and words increase activity in the brain's fear center, flooding the body with stress hormones and interrupting the logic and reasoning centers of the brain. In contrast, positive words and thoughts have the power to influence brain function, and lower physical and emotional stress.

In their book, *Words Can Change Your Brain*, authors Dr. Andrew Newberg and Mark Robert Waldman state:

*"By holding a positive and optimistic word in your mind, you stimulate frontal lobe activity. This area includes specific language centers that connect directly to the motor cortex responsible for **moving you into action** . . .*

*The longer you concentrate on positive words, the more you begin to affect other areas of the brain. Functions in the parietal lobe start to change, which **changes your perception of yourself and the people you interact with**.*

A positive view of yourself will bias you toward seeing the good in others, whereas a negative self-image will include you toward suspicion and doubt. Over time the structure of your thalamus will also change in response to your conscious words, thoughts, and feelings . . . [changing] the way in which you perceive reality" (Newberg, 2012).

Much like old woman/young girl illusion, our perception influences how we view and interact with the world. Thus, it is imperative we help our child release negative emotions and beliefs. This action

creates space in the brain to replace with positive words, thoughts, and feelings, which motivates action and generates resiliency.

We can help a child learn to let go of upsetting feelings using validation.

"Crying is how your body speaks when your mouth can't explain the pain you feel." - Unknown

Crying for Release

As a parent, if we notice our child holding back tears, we can let him or her know that crying is a normal, healthy way to express emotion. Offering a supportive shoulder to cry on while validating hurtful feelings might be exactly what our child needs to supply needed release.

Of all mammals, only humans shed tears in response to emotional stress. When a child realizes the pain he or she has been holding onto, often tears come not simply from feeling the distress, but to relieve the stress.

Crying allows both children and adults to acknowledge emotions and release them. Research shows that not only is crying natural, it's also healthy, benefitting both the body and mind in the following ways:

➤ Relieves stress - Lowers blood pressure and pulse rate.

➤ Improves mood – releases feel-good endorphins and reduces manganese, a mineral associated with anxiety, irritability and anger.

➤ Dulls pain – releases oxytocin which calms the body.

➤ Removes Toxins – eliminates chemicals like cortisol which build up during emotional stress.

➤ Self-soothes – activates the parasympathetic nervous system (PNS) which helps the body rest and digest.

➤ Rallies Support – alerts others to an urgent need for comfort and care.

➤ Restores balance – helps the body recover after experiencing any strong emotion, shifting from sadness, fear, and stress, to happiness.

Invite a child to let go of distressing emotions using visualization.

In order to communicate with the subconscious mind, where emotions and images are stored, we need to speak in a way it understands – using pictures. Studies show the subconscious brain cannot distinguish between thoughts which are real or imagined. So, whatever we imagine or intently focus on can affect or alter the emotions associated with that experience.

Children have an innate ability to create and visualize images and ideas in their minds. Utilizing this invaluable skill, we can train a child to witness releasing unwanted emotions to make space to replace with desired emotions.

Scientific studies using CAT or PET scans show that people who *IMAGINE* they are performing an action activate the same part of the brain that is involved when they actually do that action.

Whether imagining playing the piano, shooting hoops, or preparing for the Olympics, there is a mind-body connection that influences measurable change just by imagining something happening.

This means that the brain does not recognize a difference between performing and visualizing an action. Thus, closing the eyes and witnessing what you want to have happen will literally reprogram and change your brain (Kanwisher, 2000).

Harness the power of images and imagination to efficiently release distressing emotions.

Visualizations for RELEASE:

Once feelings have been **revealed**, guide a child to **release** unwanted emotions using visualization. Invite your child to sit in a comfortable chair or to lie down on a bed.

Begin by speaking the following script:

"Close your eyes. Notice in your body where you feel any uncomfortable emotions. Place your hand on your chest, stomach, or wherever you feel this feeling."

Then select a visualization from below (or choose one from Chapter 17) to complete the release.

1) **Float a Balloon**. Imagine blowing unwanted feelings (or pain) into a balloon, and tie it with a string. Notice the balloon's color before letting it go. Watch it float away, higher and farther, getting smaller and smaller until it is completely out of sight.

2) **Fall Leaves.** Imagine yourself as an autumn tree. Pretend the remaining leaves on the tree represent the feelings you want to release. Shake your body, making the leaves drop to the ground until the tree is bare. *(Optional: Finish this visualization by jumping through the leaves for fun!)*

3) **Ocean Erase**. Pretend you are writing the names of unwanted emotions in the sand with a stick. Then, watch a wave come up wash them away.

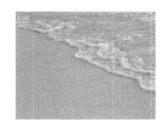

4)   **Exit Sign.** Imagine you are in a room, and the walls around you represent the distressing problem or situation. Pretend feeling faces are painted on the walls of the room. Now, imagine you can see a door with an "Exit" sign above.

Open the door, walk through, and shut the door. The problem or painful feelings have been left behind.

5)   **Drop Off a Bridge.** Imagine unwanted feelings are heavy rocks carried in a backpack. Step onto a bridge, set down the bag, and drop the rocks into a river below. Keep dropping rocks until the bag is empty.

Another version would be to invite a child to imagine holding a rock, and pouring all of the unwanted emotions from his or her body into that rock. Then, the child can envision dropping the rock into the river below.

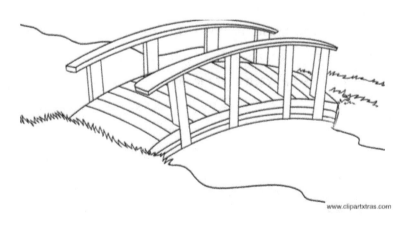

www.clipartxtras.com

Let go of unwanted feelings using validation or visualization.

Using the Validation Hero Recipe, determine the best format to release unwanted emotions:

a) Emotional self-regulation tools. Remind your child of options, such as taking a break, breathing deeply, brainstorming solutions, punching a pillow, going outside, or discharging with a shake-off.

b) Crying with comforting validation.

c) **Visualization**. Invite your child to close his or her eyes, and imagine releasing feelings from the suggested visualizations, or one of your own.

Whether allowing a child to apply self-soothing skills, or experience validating visualizations, this step allows our child to RELEASE any identified and unwanted emotions, preparing to REPLACE them with a better thought or feeling.

Tip: Win the war on whining

A child's imagination can be used to shift not only moods, but also behavior.

For example, should your child begin speaking to you with a whining voice you could reply, "Oh, my! It looks like your voice box is on the wrong setting! Let me adjust your . . . (volume, pitch, tone, etc.)." Then pick a place on the front or side of your child's neck to make a gentle switching motion.

Moreover, you could model different voices by "adjusting" your own voice box settings from high to low frequencies, different styles (opera, cowboy twang, robot, animal, etc.), or speaking in a foreign accent or language (if you have that skill).

Using humor often reduces conflict and increases cooperation, along with producing mood-shifting happiness hormones. Once your child has corrected his or her speaking voice, you can then give the necessary validation to whatever unmet need is expressed.

Chapter 16: Choose and Infuse

"Feelings are much like waves, we can't stop them from coming but we can choose which one to surf."
— Jonatan Mårtensson

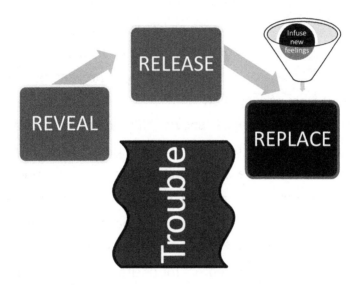

Imagine you have just purchased a brand new sports car. Pulling up to your reserved parking space, you are surprised to find an old, rusty car already parked in that spot. With no other places available, there are only two options: ram your sporty coupe into the rusty car over and over, attempting to fit into the parking spot along with it, or, remove the clunker to make room for the better vehicle.

The obvious choice is to get rid of what you don't want, and make space for something better.

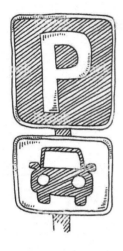

Like parking places, the brain has receptor sites for emotions which can only hold one feeling at a time. Repeated docking of strong emotions causes these sites to crave certain feelings just like a drug. This means the brain may become addicted to emotions like stress, anger, depression, or other negative feelings. These clog receptor sites, preventing better feelings from parking there.

Fortunately, science shows the brain is capable of neurogenesis, or, the creation of new brain cells and connections. As we help a child recognize or **reveal** an unwanted (or "clunker") feeling, and **release** it by applying validation or visualization, there is space to **replace it with something better**. The brain can be stimulated to create new pathways and open receptors for positive emotions to park.

After completing the first two steps of Emotional 911, our child has made SPACE TO REPLACE with a better feeling.

How do we REPLACE? By *infusing* feelings.

INFUSE means:

1) the addition of a new or necessary quality or element

2) to fill somebody with a strong emotion

3) to introduce or fix an emotion, belief, or quality firmly in somebody's mind

Choose and infuse a better thought, feeling, or belief:

Applying the power of visualization, we can invite a child to imagine the new feeling coming into his or her body or brain. This can be as simple as asking our child to pretend he or she is choosing a juice box to "drink in" the new feeling. We could invite our child to imagine being given a ball of light which represents a positive emotion, and asking where it needs to go in the body to feel better.

Why delay feeling good when it's possible to be happy right now? It's like flipping on a light switch instead of bumping around in the dark. Our child can learn that he or she has the power to "switch" to a better feeling, instead of staying stuck in the gloom.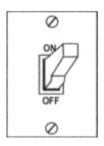

Visualizing allows our child to create emotional anchors of safety felt just as fully as if experienced in real life.

Again, the subconscious mind only understands images and emotions. This is why athletes and other high performers spend time visualizing success. They imagine what it *looks and feels* like to perfectly execute a serve, a dive, or the twists of a bobsled track.

More than just building confidence, imagination influences the subconscious mind to accept and act upon intentional instructions.

In the Disney movie, *Peter Pan*, Peter teaches the children that any happy thought will allow them to fly. In the same way, whether remembering past good experiences or dreaming of future delights, we can teach a child to tap into happier feelings to quickly shift mood.

When seeking to *REPLACE* thoughts and feelings in the subconscious, it is essential to:

1. Talk to this part of the brain in the present tense. Claim character traits and feelings by saying, "I am . . . (brave, confident, safe, happy, worthy, or loved)."

2. Be specific, focusing on what you want, not what you don't want. Eliminate negative words such as "don't" and "no" in the commands. (If we say, "Don't look at the pink elephant," the subconscious still imagines seeing an elephant.)

3. Act "as if" what you want is already happening or being felt. Pretending or imagining vividly creates cellular responses in the body. Use sensory-based language to describe how things will look and feel, as if you already have the thing you desire.

"Whatever we plant in our subconscious mind and nourish with repetition and emotion will one day become a reality." — Earl Nightingale

NAME AND REFRAME

To the body, worry, anxiety and fear generate the same sensations as excitement. A racing heart, dry mouth, butterflies in the stomach, or sweating, are signals the body is prepared for action. The body doesn't care what kind of action happens, which creates an opportunity to reframe the situation.

In a 2014 study conducted by Alison Wood Brooks at Harvard Business School, college-aged students were asked to complete a variety of stressful tasks, from singing and public speaking to math tests. Seeking to prove the power of reframing anxiety as excitement, researchers found that students performed markedly better when they were told to say, "I am excited!" or, "Get excited!" before completing the task. Those who said, "I am calm," or, "Try to stay calm," felt no decrease in stress (Brooks, 2014).

The takeaway: As a child comes to notice stress symptoms in the body, he or she can trick the mind into converting these threatening cues into feelings of excitement – like how you feel when you are winning. Instead of focusing on fearful feelings, a child can "switch" into excitement, anticipating that something good is about to happen.

Positive emotions alter gene expression, and lower both physical and emotional stress in the body. Accessing neuroplasticity (or, the ability of the brain to form new neural connections), the mind is rewired to focus on positivity.

Another brain trick is to imagine a better ending to a painful memory. In the early days of video recording, images

were stored on video tapes. These tapes could be recorded over again and again, replacing whatever had previously been recorded.

Likewise, we can invite our children to rewrite the ending of a distressing memory, thereby replacing a negative mental picture stored in their minds. This time, they can imagine being given a superpower, or they can select a secret weapon to help alter the outcome. Some children choose an invisibility cloak, so they can go unnoticed by a bully. Others choose shields  to protect themselves, or wings to quickly move away from danger.

Another option is to give your child a "Brave Button" or a "Safety Stone" to keep in their pocket. Like Dumbo's Magic Feather, a real or imagined object can carry your child over troubled waters. Infuse the object with the desired or needed emotion, such as courage, peace, or safety. Ask your child if they can feel that new emotion emanating from the gift. If not, encourage them to rub the item back and forth like a genie's lamp to "activate" the energy.

Metaphors or analogies are effective imagery for replacing feelings and beliefs:

The following are samples from client sessions using the 3-step sequence of Emotional 911: Reveal, Release, and Replace.

Chip came to see me at the age of 44 with PTSD symptoms after serving two tours of duty in the military. He felt stuck in the past, and we revealed his fearful belief, "I don't know how to protect myself." Yet, underneath his tough exterior, there was a broken little boy needing validation from an earlier pain point in life.

Chip grew up in a family of five kids, and was four years old when his mom abandoned the family, leaving him feeling forgotten, discarded, and alone. His father was molesting his older sisters, and when Chip was nine years old, a sister began molesting him. This younger Chip felt enraged, empty, and filled with shame. He said the feelings felt like a pile of logs jammed in a river, reducing the flow to a trickle.

I invited Chip to imagine he was removing a log for each feeling we released, until the river was open and flowing again. When that was done, he said he felt safe and strong. I then invited Chip to replace his former, broken belief with something better. Chip chose: "I am able to protect the people I love."

A high school sophomore, Nick felt deeply depressed comparing his abilities to others'. This left him feeling weak, worthless, and small by comparison. After revealing and releasing unhealthy feelings, we were ready to reprogram his subconscious using imagery. I asked Nick how he wanted to feel instead. He said "hopeful, included, and happy."

215

Knowing Nick belonged to a swim team, I invited him to imagine diving into a pool of those positive feelings. Next, I

asked him visualize swimming a race, and notice what happened if he looked to the side or backward. He said looking around at others actually slowed him down. This helped Nick realize that the contest was against his best efforts, not against others.

We infused motivation--a new feeling for Nick--with the understanding of how to improve without comparing. Nick was able to identify his unique abilities and recognize his responsibility to develop them. He was able to accept that we each have different talents, but that the blessing for sharing them (versus burying them) is the same for all: an increase! Nick said he felt peaceful, hopeful, and able to see himself connecting with others claiming, "I am worthy and valued."

Twelve-year-old Landon struggled with OCD (Obsessive Compulsive Disorder.) Whether real or imagined, he feared coming into contact with things that would make him feel dirty, and then ritually washing his hands or showering. He said the compelling thoughts, triggered by fear of being contaminated or contaminating places by simply being there, were like a train that had already left the station. At that point, he felt like he had no control over where the train would take him.

In our session, I invited him to imagine what he could do to regain control of the train. Could he create a "Stop" button inside the train car, or a way to escape? After thinking about it, Landon suggested installing a lever that would allow him to switch the train to a different track, and change the destination to a happy place instead of "Contamination Land." In his mind, he could use this switch to manage his thoughts and choose something better.

One of my favorite replacing metaphors is the "Heart Protector." In our session, Kacie reported struggling in her relationship with her sister, saying, "No one hurts me more than she does. Sometimes I feel stabbed through the heart."

After identifying feeling hopeless, hurt, betrayed, and abused, we imagined a conversation where Kacie asked forgiveness for her part in their struggles, and Kacie forgave her sister for past hurts.

Kacie was worried about how she would respond to future interactions with her sister, so I invited Kacie to imagine a "Heart Protector."

Like a child's shape-sorter toy where the circle can only go

in the circle hole, and a triangle in the *triangle spot, Kacie imagined that the* *only "shape" she could receive in her* *heart was love--loving words and* *actions. Nothing else could get* *through that heart-shaped opening,* *which allowed her to feel safe* *interacting with her sister and others.*

Kacie went home and taught the imagery to her grade-school son, who had experienced some bullying at school. It became a tender, shared metaphor which opened further support and communication. Together they claimed: "I am protected and safe."

Once a child has visualized releasing unwanted feelings, there is space to replace and receive something better.

I often invite clients to imagine that they see a treasure box, and can select a gift from inside in order to claim a better

feeling. Most of the contents chosen are just ordinary objects.

Then, I invite them to tell me what the gift means to them, and any new beliefs or feelings they notice.

Below is a list of imaginary gifts chosen by clients during visualization to "replace."

The intent is to offer a tool to overcome past challenges, find peace in the present, and *claim new feelings* to face the future.

Once a gift is selected, ask what that object represents. Should a child be unsure of an item's meaning, brainstorm together some possible interpretations.

- Paddleball Game—"I am safe to try and have fun! If I miss the ball, it's still attached by a string, and I can try again. I can gain skill while I play."

- Globe--giving me the world and permission to do or become anything I want.

- Fire-Breathing Dragon--to give myself a voice. "I have the power to say, 'No!'"

- Pink Pearl Eraser--permission to make mistakes.

- Diving Board--keep trying as many times as it takes.

- Guitar—reclaiming my voice.

- Hat—provides protection (from negative thoughts).

- Snowflake—"I am unique, but I belong."

- Key--opens the door to possibilities.

- Ferris Wheel--spins easily, allowing "new" to be let on, and "old" to be released.

REPLACE

Choose and infuse a better feeling.

Once a child has imagined releasing unwanted feelings, there is space to replace and receive something better.

A) Identify the intended emotions or desired beliefs to replace.

B) Allow the replacement or infusion of healthier feelings. Reprogram the subconscious using a mental picture, story, or metaphor to anchor that new feeling.

C) From that point forward, speak and act "as if" you already feel the emotions you desire using positive, "I am . . . (*excited, brave, smart, safe, loved, etc.*)" statements.

Imagination is like time travel; it can take us to the past and the future. Visualizations allow a child to repair or heal previous pain points, and then claim better beliefs and feelings to move forward into the future.

Chapter 17: Feel Better Fast

"We must accept finite disappointment,
but we must never lose infinite hope."
- Martin Luther King

When first responders show up at the scene of an emergency, they don't come empty-handed. Not knowing what will be needed, they carry a variety of tools and come ready to tackle whatever crisis they may face. From communication and monitoring devices, to medical and protective gear, they arrive prepared to give aid.

Similarly, part of Emotional 911 involves knowing how to respond to a child's emotional emergencies. Amid a "feeling storm," it can be difficult to calm our child. We must come prepared with healing tools and  practices to provide immediate assistance.

First things first; any emergency responder will make sure the person in crisis is breathing. When in distress, a child's breathing may change. Whether hyperventilating or holding their breath, we can encourage our child (and ourselves) to take slow, deep breaths THROUGH THE NOSE to calm the body.

Gasping, or mouth breathing, activates a fight/flight/freeze response (sympathetic) in the body. Breathing deeply through the nose accesses the lower lobes of the lungs, which are loaded with calming (parasympathetic) receptor sites, and increases alpha-wave production in the brain, calming the nervous system. This allows a child to become physically and emotionally present to name and tame what is causing pain.

Next, just as a wise parent will have a first aid kit on hand with medicines, bandages and balms, a tangible emotional first aid kit offers tools our child can access when a feeling crisis strikes.

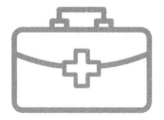 **Select a calm time to create an emotional first aid kit a child can reach for in times of distress.**

Creating a kit could involve brainstorming with a child for a list of self-soothing or calming activities. Place slips of paper suggesting ways to feel better fast in a jar, such as: getting outside, calling a friend, or cuddling on the couch. The notes might include items from a self-care list such as: breathing deeply, petting an animal, or having a shake-it-off dance party. (Parents don't be shy about applying the suggestions for your own stress relief, as well.)

Younger children may need touchable objects to remind them of emotional first aid options. Fill a box or a backpack with items, such as: a squeeze-ball to diffuse distress, a balloon for blowing away unwanted emotions, or a plastic dinosaur toy, which suggests stomping out stressful feelings.

Consider adding a whiteboard with dry erase markers, or a notebook with colored pencils. Add pictures (of family or favorite places), craft supplies (like pipe cleaners), bubbles (to blow away unwanted feelings), and dolls or action figures. Tuck in appropriate "feeling" books or games.

The goal is not simply to distract our child from distressing emotions, but to provide tools with which our child can emote.

In addition to preparing an emotional first aid kit, be ready with healing practices to assist a child through the Emotional 911 Sequence.

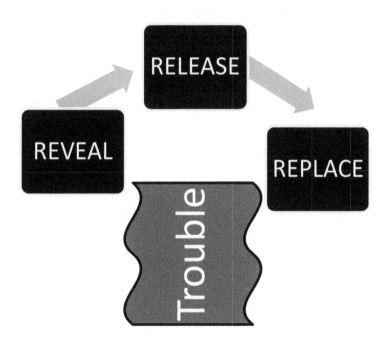

Begin with the Validation Hero Recipe **to help a child identify whatever is causing distress.** Complete the process by applying one of the following visualization tools below:

BALLOON FLOAT

REVEAL: Help your child name what is being felt (start with sad, angry, guilty, or afraid) using the Validation Hero Recipe.

RELEASE: Invite your child to close their eyes and imagine

holding a deflated balloon. Ask him/her to give three deep puffs, just as you would to inflate a balloon, filling the balloon with the unwanted feelings. Have him/her imagine tying off the balloon, and ask what color he/she sees.

(Note: Colors often correspond to the rainbow hues of chakras or energy centers in the body, but simply naming the color makes the mental picture more vivid.)

Then, invite your child to imagine letting the balloon go, and watching it float up into the sky until it fades from view. Once the unwanted balloon is gone . . .

REPLACE: Have your child visualize receiving a new balloon on a string, or an imaginary lollipop, asking your child to identify what new feeling they choose to infuse.

OPERATION

Have your child to pretend they can see a picture where their body is mapped out like the board game *OPERATION,* by Milton Bradley.

REVEAL: Invite your child to describe the location and look (color or shape) the pain has. Seek to discover the feelings causing that pain and validate them.

RELEASE: Then, invite your child to imagine using tweezers to remove the unwanted shape.

REPLACE: Choose a better feeling to instill by putting a new color or shape into that opening.

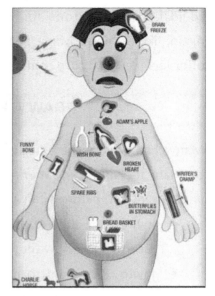

SKIP A STONE

Invite your child to imagine they are holding a rock.

REVEAL: After naming any unwanted feelings, suggest your child make a fist and push all of the anger, sadness, or other distressing feelings into that rock or stone.

RELEASE: Invite your child to pretend dropping that rock off of a bridge, or skipping that stone across the water. Have him or her watch for the splash, or count the skips until the stone sinks under the water.

REPLACE: Suggest your child imagine being given a new stone in which you put a better or desired positive emotion from your reserves.

The opposite of a "worry stone," this real or imagined rock could be a touch-stone for whatever emotion is required. Again, like Dumbo's Magic Feather, this imaginary object can offer feelings for future confidence or comfort.

DRAW A PICTURE

Many children lack the emotional vocabulary to describe how they are feeling after experiencing something distressing or unpleasant, yet, pictures can give us important clues:

- Invite your child to draw a self-portrait with a feeling face to show how they feel, or
- Invite your child to draw an object that represents them. Look for clues given by the type of object drawn, or perhaps items that are missing or broken.

Remember to use the follow-up question, "How do you feel?" in order to reveal, release, and replace distressing emotions.

One 10-year-old client drew a picture of herself with no arms, even though the rest of the body was very detailed. When asked about the missing arms, she said they were tied behind her back. This opened further discussion about where she was feeling helpless in her life.

Another client, age 16, drew a picture of a glass with a large crack down the front. When asked what the crack represented, she replied, "I'm damaged goods." Identifying this broken belief allowed her to share some abuse that needed validation and healing.

JOURNAL

REVEAL. Limit "worry time" to a few minutes each day. Set a timer for five to ten minutes, and invite your child to write down everything they are worried about on a paper until the timer goes off. If they are in a pre-writing stage, you can write fears down for  your child as they tell them to you. Often, the process of getting the concerns down on paper minimizes or frees fears from the body and mind.

RELEASE the worries by making the paper into a ball or ripping it into pieces to toss into the trash.

REPLACE concerns by inviting your child to engage in a physical activity or drawing positive word art on a paper to claim new emotions.

For older children and teens, encourage your child to look at the list of worries, and identify any of the items that could be resolved or eased by action. Then, help your child determine one thing he or she could do, including asking someone for help, for each of these needs.

Caution: Briefly writing about anxious feelings can alleviate those symptoms temporarily. However, regularly journaling negative thoughts and feelings can increase anxiety and depression. Be sure "worry writings" are replaced with positivity, such as claiming a better feeling, or creating a gratitude journal. After just three weeks of recording good moments, most youth report more satisfaction with life, hope, and optimism (Emmons, 2003).

CHALKBOARD ERASE

No paper? No problem. You can also create a worry or "distressing feelings" list on an imaginary chalkboard:

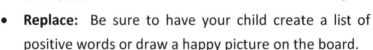

- **Reveal:** Ask your child to imagine writing unwanted feelings, or adding unhappy emoticons, to a chalkboard.
- **Release:** Invite your child to pretend to erase everything on the board.
- **Replace:** Be sure to have your child create a list of positive words or draw a happy picture on the board.

FILL AND DUMP

Whether playing with buckets of sand or bins of toys, most children love to fill containers, dump them out, and fill them again. We can use this common concept to have a child imagine that he or she has a container filled with distressing emotions. Next, invite your child to dump out the unwanted emotions, and choose a better feeling to load into the bucket.

The same premise works by imagining a bathtub filled with liquid, representing the unwanted emotions. Invite your child to pull the plug and watch the liquid drain completely out. Then, refill the tub with a fun bubble bath of happy feelings.

HEARTLIGHT

Fear triggers two innate core fears--fear of failure (thinking we are not good enough), or fear of loss (being afraid we won't have or get what we need). Psychiatrist and author, Elisabeth Kubler-Ross explains,

> "There are only two primary emotions: love and fear. Love makes us feel safe, worthy, and 'enough.' All positive emotions come from love, all negative emotions from fear. From love flows happiness, contentment, peace and joy.
>
> From fear comes anger, hate, anxiety and guilt. But it's more accurate to say that **there is only love OR fear, for we cannot feel these two emotions together, at exactly the same time**. They're opposites. If we're in fear, we are not in a place of love. When we are in a place of love, we cannot be in a place of fear" (Kubler-Ross, 2000).

Since we can only feel the emotion of love *or* fear, we can invite our child to imagine having an outlet-shaped plug located in the heart.

- **Reveal** distressing or fearful emotions, and choose a shape to imagine for the unwanted nightlight plugged into the heart outlet.
- **Release.** Unplug and discard (or destroy) the undesired light.
- **Replace.** Create a new nightlight shape. Infuse this light with love and any additional desired feelings (such as happy, brave, or "enough") to plug into the heart.

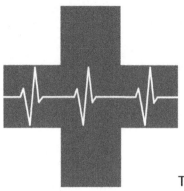

Tangible items can be added to an emotional first aid kit to represent any of these guided visualizations. Consider adding a balloon, bubbles, tweezers, a rock, a journal, or a drawing board to trigger a visualization method to try.

Just as one type of bandage doesn't work in every situation, different styles of Emotional 911 imagery will resonate more strongly with one child than another. You may find a certain approach more effective, or recognize your child needs a variety of tools, depending on the level of emotional first aid required.

Emotional 911

Like putting ice on a burn or removing a splinter, our child will come to seek the instant relief felt from employing emotional first aid. As we routinely repeat the healing pattern of Emotional 911, the steps will become second nature.

Eventually, our child will be able to access and address his or her own emotional wounds, revealing feelings as they surface, and applying visualization skills to release and then replace with better feelings and beliefs.

Chapter 18: Attics and iPhones

"Memory is the diary we all carry about with us."
- Oscar Wilde

Most homes are built with an attic - the triangular space below the roof with exposed trusses and sloped walls. The room typically isn't good for anything but storage, becoming a receptacle for baby items, seasonal decorations, and memorabilia we just can't part with.

Long before modular shelving and three-car garages, families would store souvenirs and stacks of letters, pictures and personal items in trunks and boxes for each following generation. Forgotten high school yearbooks offered a snapshot  into fashion and fads of times gone. Old diaries would report on life's everyday activities and adventures. Most of these treasures, along with some useless trash, lay tucked away until a death, move, or curiosity triggered their discovery.

For humans, the brain serves as an attic for life experiences.

Memories aren't stored in just one part of the brain. Instead, information is tucked into different corners of interconnecting regions, depending on the type of memory.

Episodic or event memories are autobiographical, recorded from *our* perspective of what we experience. Other spots of the brain store semantic memories, such as general facts and information, which are indexed for future access. The brain has special locations for working memory, habit formation, motor activity, learning, and reward processing.

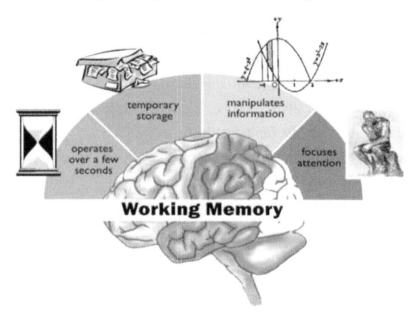

In an almond-shaped region of the brain called the amygdala, **emotional significance is attached to each individual experience, helping the brain to sort events by importance.** Like the characters from Disney's movie, *Inside Out,* memories associated with strong emotions such as joy, shame, love, or grief are sorted for survival information and stored.

Memories are either hidden away in the subconscious or featured so we can't forget.

Beyond our own cache of memories, we inherit collectibles from previous generations. Recent genetic research shows that trauma, *when unresolved*, creates thought programs and behavior responses that affect not only the individual personally, but transfer from generation to generation. This means, just like family heirlooms and memories stored in an attic, our brain holds not only *our memories,* but also the coding of survival beliefs and instructions from *our ancestors.*

Scientists call this programming "epigenetics," and it includes features that are "on top of" inherited genetic information. These epigenetic expressions can manifest as weaknesses or strengths, rigidity or resilience.

So, what does that mean for us personally?

While you might have inherited grandma's gift of gab, you may also end up duplicating your dad's debilitating depression.

Along with temperament traits, we inherit limiting or broken beliefs (like the list in Chapter 3) which may trigger feeling powerless or compelled. For good or bad, this epigenetic encoding handcuffs us to our forebears' history. Unless remedied, these programs may saddle not only ourselves, but also future generations with unresolved pain, influencing:

- mental illness and substance addiction
- physical disease
- relationship or parenting styles
- memory acquisition, and
- emotional resilience

"According to the new insights of behavioral epigenetics, traumatic experiences in our past, or in our recent ancestors' past, leave molecular scars adhering to our DNA. Jews whose great-grandparents were chased from their Russian shtetlekh [villages]; Chinese whose grandparents lived through the ravages of the Cultural Revolution; young immigrants from Africa whose parents survived massacres; adults of every ethnicity who grew up with alcoholic or abusive parents — all carry with them more than just memories.

Like silt deposited on the cogs of a finely-tuned machine after the seawater of a tsunami recedes, our experiences, and those of our ancestors, are never gone even if they have been forgotten. They become a part of us; a molecular residue holding fast to our genetic scaffolding. The DNA remains the same, but psychological and behavioral tendencies are inherited. You might have inherited not just your grandmother's knobby knees, but also her predisposition toward depression caused by the neglect she suffered as a newborn.

Or not. If your grandmother was adopted by nurturing parents, you might be enjoying the boost she received thanks to their love and support.

The genome has long been known as the blueprint of life, but the epigenome is life's Etch-A-Sketch; shake it hard enough, and you can wipe clean the family curse"

- Grandma's Experience Leaves a Mark on Your Genes, (Hurley, 2013).

Smartphone Epigenome

To understand the relationship of DNA (our hereditary genetic coding) and epigenetics, consider this analogy:

Imagine DNA as a Smartphone, and the epigenome as the programs that come pre-loaded onto that device. Some programs will initiate at birth, running silently in the background, such as physical sensitivities, making one prone to allergies, or immune response malfunctions.

Other beliefs and programs are like loaded icons just waiting for critical events or stress to "double-tap" them into activation. Given the right genetic and environmental factors, troubling or traumatic events may trigger pre-loaded, negative thought patterns and beliefs from our ancestors.

These can become dominant drivers in our behavior, and can include stress-reaction programs like anxiety, depression, and anger. Often, these undesirable icons gobble up valuable memory space and prevent us from loading desired applications, or good things we do want in our lives.

Fortunately, the Emotional 911 Sequence allow us to:

- address ancestral molecular scars adhering to our DNA, and
- triage and treat wounds from our own troubling life experiences.

Recognizing unhealthy responses or noticing nonsense beliefs that don't feel like "ours," we can delete unwanted applications using the EMOTIONAL 911 sequence, as we:

- **Reveal** emotional pain points, broken beliefs, or program applications with the Validation Hero Recipe.

- **Release** the emotions and beliefs as you imagine holding a finger on an unwanted program until the icon shakes, and then "X-ing" it out of existence. This frees up valuable storage space.

- **Replace** or upload new, healthier operating instructions from an imaginary "app store" full of unlimited possibilities.

Struggles of feeling like, "I don't fit in," or self-sabotaging behaviors we notice in our child may remind us of similar battles from our own growing-up years. We want things to be different, better, or easier for our child, yet generational broken beliefs can restrict potential until they are resolved.

Emotional 911 is imperative, not only attending to the present wounding of our child, but also salving sore spots in our personal past, and repairing pain points of previous generations.

In my work with clients, it's not uncommon for me to see multiple members of the same family. Sometimes, sisters will refer each other. Other times, a parent who has mended past pain points will want his or her child to feel the same relief. This is where unhealthy patterns of behavior, based on generational beliefs, become plainly evident.

Betty underwent a bitter divorce 10 years ago, but still found herself living with resentment and anger toward her ex-husband. Listing all the ways things were not fair, she professed, "Nothing goes my way." After helping her identify unhealthy emotions and apply emotional first aid, she was able to, "Let go and let God."

Shortly thereafter, she scheduled a session for her 18-year-old son, Ryan, who was depressed over circumstances in his life. Recently wrecking his car, losing his job, and being dumped by his girlfriend left him feeling defeated and humiliated. Listing all the things going wrong in his life, Ryan reported, "Nothing goes my way."

I was fascinated as both mother and son described their interpretation of life events with the exact same phrase. Identifying this as a broken *generational* belief, we worked through the Emotional 911 process to reveal, release, and replace the ensuing emotions with preferred feelings.

During the steps of Ryan's release and replace, I invited him to imagine what a cell phone icon would look like for the belief, "Nothing goes my way." He told me he could imagine

seeing a dark, grey frowning face. I asked him to envision holding his finger on the icon until it started shaking, and then hitting the "X" in the corner to delete the program.

Once that was done, I invited him to choose a new program to upload. Ryan claimed the belief that, "Life is good." He imagined the icon being a happy face on a bright, yellow background. He said, "When you tap open the app, it tells you positive messages like, 'Everything is going to be okay,' and 'You have to do the work, but it will pay off.' The app also reminds you to ask, 'Why do things work out so good for me?'"

These better beliefs have allowed Ryan to move forward with hope and optimism. The circumstances did not have to change for him to be happy, because he had changed.

Attending to emotional wounds and past pain points isn't just about finding relief; it's about finding re-life.

Webster defines the prefix "re-" as, "*again or anew.*" Healing our emotional injuries, and those of our children, frees us from limiting thoughts and debilitating emotions, *renewing* our ability to move forward in the direction of our dreams.

Applying validation, along with the Emotional 911 Sequence, allows us to hold hands not only with our child, but across generations, providing the healing and peace we all seek.

Afterword by Megan Bryant

When I was in the 4th grade, I ran for vice president of our elementary school in the student body elections. My opponent was Tyler Jorgensen. He was also, at the time, one of my first big crushes. Oh boy, was he cuuuuuuute! I wanted to win to impress him, yet I wanted him to win because he was handsome and smart and cool, and I want others to succeed. I made a rookie mistake during the elections, and I voted for Tyler. I assumed that was the admirable thing. He probably did the same for me, right? Wrong. You gotta vote for yourself in an election, friends, otherwise, what are you even doing there?

I lost the election. I had my first bitter taste of defeat. I sat in the hallway outside the classroom with my mother next to me. She sat quietly with her arm around me, as I cried my eyes out for a good, long, excruciating six minutes. That is the first time I can recall feeling a flood of conflicting and overwhelming emotions simultaneously. I was embarrassed for losing. I was sad. I wanted to quit school because obviously *nobody liked me*. At the same time, I was feeling happy for Tyler. I saw his big smile. He looked so proud. And he was kind to me after his victory and sensitive to my feelings as the loser.

My mom listened to me blubber. She told me how proud of me she was. She allowed me space to feel so many feelings without judgment or pressure to "control" them, and without trying to navigate them for me. I have always felt safe to experience emotions with her because of her willingness to love me and support me, validating my emotions no matter where they fell on the spectrum.

Now, as a divorced/single mother of four young children, I can't help but feel a tremendous amount of responsibility for the health and happiness of these rapidly-forming "humanlings." At present, they are ages ten, five, three, and twenty months. Three of them are boys, and the five-year-old is my girl. They are glorious young people, filled with energy and potential, and I don't want to screw them up!

On September 15, 2017, 16 years of marriage had ended. The divorce was final. The story of the ups and downs and wild ride of that marriage is enough to fill a book of its own, but the short version is that it was not possible to salvage the relationship.

The plan, as parents of very young children, was to cohabitate in the home that we lived in so the kids wouldn't feel such an abrupt change. That arrangement was short-lived, as I felt a *very* strong prompting that I was not in a safe space to begin healing emotionally. Rental homes were hard to come by, but that next morning, the perfect fit plopped directly in my lap. And it was available right away.

The week we moved out, it all came to a head. All the volatility of the human emotions that are attached to grief and sadness hit like a freight train.

Immediately, in that transitional time, we all became physically ill. All five of us began an aggressive rotation of vomiting and diarrhea. There were minimal signs of any identifiable illnesses. Spotty fevers here and there, but otherwise, the kids were their usual energetic selves, but would not be able to go more than a handful of hours without somebody throwing up.

Around the clock.

Days passed.

Then weeks.

No sign of improvement.

Doctors kept telling me the kids were fine; all tests were clear. They were not fine.

I checked with friends and family for suggestions. I was concerned about food allergies suddenly developing. Perhaps this home had health concerns. I had the local firefighters come to test the home for carbon monoxide poisoning. I'd had a severe loss of appetite altogether, while the kids just simply couldn't keep anything down. Not even water.

My mom was around to help me a lot. We did so much laundry; bedding and towels, the outfits that had been thrown-up on, and then, cleaning the carpets. It would happen without notice; just kids, laughing and playing, and then suddenly vomiting, or filling another diaper. I could hardly sleep at night. It had gotten to where there hadn't been a single night where I didn't bolt awake because of the sound of heaving, and race to catch as much as possible in one of the bowls that had been strategically placed. The kids were scared and crying. I reassured them that we were all okay, and we'd get cleaned up.

"Everything will be okay." A phrase I said on repeat for those grueling months.

Several unsuccessful doctor visits later, including a visit to the emergency room with my daughter for fluids--and with no sign of relief in sight--I felt hopeless. I'd been tending to vomiting children and explosive bowel movements for so long, I wondered if I'd ever smell anything other than the sour, bitter fragrance of sickness.

No prescriptions had helped to rid our home of this malady. At long last, the children's pediatrician attributed this all to the extreme, fast-paced shifts the kids and I were navigating together. He prescribed counseling for the older children, and talked me through some additional steps to try and keep the calm, reassuring, stable expectations in my own home.

I have always believed that a body's physical well-being is closely woven with its emotions, but this was just too much. *How could I fix this?*

On December 6th, after nearly two solid months of sickness, I reached out to Laura Sonderegger, knowing her experience and expertise in emotional "clearing." I had messaged her out of desperation.

Understanding that our emotions are so critical to our physical health, I trusted that this call with Laura would be helpful. We were only on the phone for about a half hour.

All four kids were home, and busy as usual. I scrambled a bit to find a quiet place to focus. I retreated to my bedroom upstairs, closed the door, and sat on the floor. In our session, we didn't focus on the details of how the divorce was affecting the kids and myself, but the private elements of how I was feeling. Then, with my eyes closed, Laura quietly walked me through a very intentional and personal visualization.

I imagined allowing Christ to be the buffer between me and the hurt feelings I had from the divorce. It was to allow Him to step in and say, "I'm sorry," on behalf of those who never would on their own. To focus on Him when trials hit. To allow Him to take those pains upon His shoulders.

After I'd pondered on Him and allowed Him to step in as a teammate on this journey, Laura shifted the visual elements. She invited me to imagine a set of Russian nesting dolls. She asked me to open them up, one by one, with each doll representing one of my children. Then, to place a ball of light, symbolizing love and healing, into each of them before returning the tops back onto each doll. I did so.

Laura then paused and asked, "When you opened the dolls, did you un-stack them, or did the bases stay stacked inside the larger dolls?" I replied that I had left them nested during that exercise. She explained to me that the word "responsibility" came up for me, which came as no surprise. I often feel responsible for making other people happy, and for taking care of them first, and letting my own needs simmer on the backburner, or, get completely cold and crusty on the stove of life.

Quite firmly but lovingly, Laura reinforced that I need only accept responsibility for those things within my control; within my new household, while these children are in my direct care. Everything else will be what it will be. She tied this all together for me and then we concluded the call.

That night was the greatest purge of all. I was the one hanging my head over the toilet at least once an hour all night long. Visits throughout the night were dry heaves and tears. I've never felt so weak and tired in all my life, even compared to delivering five babies.

Around 1am, I called my mom and asked for her to come. I was afraid that if any of my children needed me, I would be unable to even lift them. She came straight away and stayed through that following afternoon.

Then it was over.

The vomiting.

The diarrhea.

For all of us.

After two months, within less than a 24-hour cycle, there was no more of any of it. The clock kept ticking. Still no bodily fluids raged from one end or the other. The food and drinks began to cycle through our bodies as normal. My kids cheered each time they had a solid bowel movement. I cheered. I wept with absolute happiness and relief.

It all finally happened because I allowed myself to un-hitch from the situation in a way that would allow me to move forward, taking ownership of my own life; to lift my head to the sky and inhale the freedom we all have access to if we let our Savior do His job. I allowed love to take the wheel and steer all my decisions of how I react to things.

Laura never took credit for this amazing experience. She simply delights in the opportunity to help other people channel their energy in a better direction, and to offer relief to those who need to unpack very, very, heavy emotional backpacks. She loves people, and most importantly, she loves for people to feel that love at a level that seems super human, because the power of a loving Heavenly Father and our Savior, Jesus Christ, is greater than anything else in existence.

As a parent, I need to be healthy and take care of myself physically and emotionally, so that I can be in tune with the physical and emotional needs of my children. My own emotional overwhelm had me by the throat, as so many life-altering events were happening simultaneously.

Thankfully, Laura helped me sort through those feelings in a simple, practical way, so I could step back into my own power and capacity to live as an engaging, strong woman. And, as a result, be empowered to be a beacon of light and strength for my kids, and help them find healing, too.

Megan Bryant
Award-Winning Author, Comedian, Corporate Trainer
http://www.meetmeganbryant.com

Resources

Self-Validation
Hero Recipe

Ouch! That hurts.

W
- Worst
- What's the worst part?

I
- Identify
- How do *I* feel?

N
- Need
- What do *I* need?

Will I be okay?

Validation
Hero Recipe

I'm Sorry...

W	• Worst • What's the worst part?
I	• Identify • How do you feel?
N	• Need • What do you need?

Will you be okay?

The Emotional 911 Sequence

1) Reveal: Name and Tame

Identify or name the feeling as it surfaces

2) Release: Feel and Deal

Let go of unwanted feelings using validation and visualization

3) Replace: Choose and Infuse

Name and claim a better feeling, thought, or belief

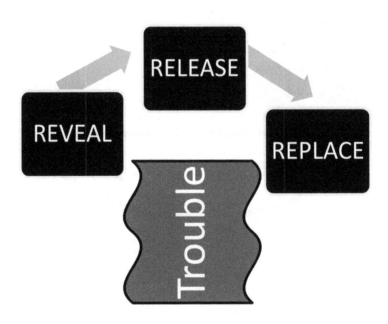

Feeling Faces Grid

Illustrations
by Aubree Hope

	A	B	C	D
1	Excited	Loved	Content	Happy
2	Sad	Angry	Guilty	Afraid
3	Shocked	Ashamed	Hurt	Worried
4	Lonely	Surprised	Confused	Frustrated
5	Unable	Unloved	Unsafe	Unfair

Note: Use of feeling grids can be enhanced using Applied Kinesiology or "muscle testing" to pinpoint non-conscious distressing emotions. This is a skill anyone can learn, but is beyond the scope of this book.

Feeling Words Grid

Presenting Problem			
Relates to person or situation?			

Mom	Dad	Sibling	Relative	Work	School	Team	Church
Teacher	Friend	Peer	Other	Illness	Money	Work	Other

Relates to which blocked emotions?			
A	**B**	**C**	**D**
1 Sad	Angry	Guilty	Afraid
2 Abandoned Abused Alone	Annoyed Bad Bitter	Avoidance Awful Blame	Anxious Hurt Intimidated
3 Cheated Confused Depressed	Blocked Critical Disappointed	Defensive Disgust Distrust	Lost Overwhelmed Panic
4 Frustrated Heartbroken Helpless	Discouraged Dumb Embarrassed	Doubtful Dread Forgetful	Scared Stuck Surprised
5 Hesitant Hopeless Homesick	Failure Forced Forgetful	Indecisive Inferior Insecurity	Terrified Threatened Trapped
6 Humiliated Insecure Left Out	Hatred Ignored Jealous	Irresponsible Judgmental Naughty	Unprotected Unsupported Unsuccessful
7 Lonely Nervous Shy	Resentful Restricted Rejected	Not enough Responsible Self-rejected	Unworthy Unsafe Unloved
8 Tired Ugly Unhappy	Shocked Surprised Stifled	Shame Stubborn Stupid	Unloveable Unwanted Violated
9 Uncomfortable Unnoticed Worried	Rushed Unappreciated Unfair	Powerless Unable Unimportant	Vulnerable Weak Worthless

Body Metaphor Messages

Symptom	Possible Message
Acne	Taking things personally. *What can't you face?*
ADD/ADHD	Scattered thoughts and energy. Connections are uncomfortable. Belief: I must keep moving. *What will happen if you don't?*
Addiction	Physical result of the desire to avoid pain or run away from truth, from life, from responsibilities.
Allergies	*Who or what is irritating you?*
Ankles	Lack of assurance; can't decide on best course of action.
Anxiety	Inability to reconcile the inside with the outside. There is a sense of overwhelm and uncertainty.
Back	Feeling unsupported.
Bi-Polar	Seemingly never ending cycle of extreme self-hatred and self-approval. "I can't do anything right" cycles to "I can do everything and rules don't apply to me."
Bladder	Ability to cleanse and release that which is no longer needed.
Cough	Suppressed thoughts or emotions.
Depression	Belief that things will never get better.
Digestion	Ability to process (or digest) thoughts and feelings. *What feels out of your control?*
Ears	*What don't you want to hear?*
Eyes	*What don't you want to see?*

Symptom	Possible Message
Feet	How we feel about moving forward.
Fingers	How we feel about our ability to grasp what is happening.
Hands	How we feel about our work. *What experiences are you holding onto that need to be released?*
Heart	Ability to sustain oneself. Can be a reflection of emotional difficulties within family. Feeling of lack connected to grief, pain, heartbreak, despair or hatred.
Knees	Fear of bending to authority. Pressure to perform.
Legs	How we carry ourselves forward. Lacking direction or trust in choices.
Muscle Pain	Indecision about whether to hold on or let go of an issue; unsure which choice is safe.
Neck	How we deal with differing viewpoints. *Who or what is a pain in the neck?*
Nose	Represents tolerance/intolerance.
Overweight	Inability or unwillingness to express one's emotions. Habitually using food to soothe emotions. *What makes you feel unsafe?*
OCD	Doing a behavior is often preferable to trying to express one's dissatisfaction with authority.
Pain	Exists as a way to let us know we are in emotional or spiritual pain, and have unrecognized or unresolved issues. For some, feeling physical pain is the only way to express emotional needs.
Posture	Can reveal how one is feeling.

Symptom	*Possible Message*
Pelvis	Belief: feelings terrify me.
Self-mutilation	A silent plea for help or attention. Wanting to show one's pain in the world. Chronic distress.
Shoulders	Represents burdens; unable or unwilling to take or release responsibility. Feeling overwhelmed.
Sleep disorders	*Insomnia:* trying to avoid thinking about something or trying to remember everything. Feeling unsafe to let one's guard down. *Night Terrors:* Fear, insecurity *Sleep-walking:* Trying to run away (abandonment, avoidance).
Solar Plexus (gut)	Thought to be your power center. Pain or tightness in this area generally indicates fear, worry, or nervousness.
Spine	Represents feelings regarding being supported or stuck.
Throat	Self-expression. Suppressing a strong feeling.
Warts	Belief that one is unworthy or fear one is useless.

Body and Illness Messages lists adapted from *Physical Conditions and their Spiritual Components* (McBeath, 2018).

Illness Emotional Messages

Symptom	Possible Message
Abscess	Festering of past hurts. Feeling resentment, disappointment.
Asthma	Regularly responding to the unknown with confusion, agitation, anxiety, fear, panic or distrust; can be a means of controlling a tense situation.
Athlete's foot	Impatient: always in a hurry
Bronchitis	Feeling forced into being the responsible one and angry about it; Under-appreciated.
Chickenpox	Wanting to be like everybody else.
Colds	Caused by virus. *Where do you feel unworthy or not good enough?*
Constipation	Represents an inability to let go.
Diabetes	Lack of faith or hope that the future can be good. In children, can occur after the family receives a devastating blow. Disappointment/Lack of joy.
Diarrhea	Feeling like someone is trying to make you hurry.
Earache	Distress about one's environment. *What don't you want to hear?*
Flu	Often comes when one is about to be tested and fears failing, or to avoid commitments.
Hand-foot-mouth	Chronic unmet need for attention from caregiver or authority figure.
Headaches	Often an excuse to escape responsibility. Never enough time. Possible emotions: distress, worry, confusion, & avoidance.

Symptom	Possible Message
Hypochondria	Wanting to steal attention from others (envy) or avoid responsibilities. A chronic need to be in crisis.
Infection	Can occur when one feels that one's desires are constantly being denied. Believing, "I never get what I want," or "When is it going to be my turn?"
Measles	Fear of the unknown, fear of invasion; fear that nothing will ever improve.
Mumps	Afraid of taking the next step.
Nasal Drip	Crying silently so nobody can see or hear it, but hoping someone will notice.
Stomach	Worried what you say/do is wrong.
Polio	Wanting the family to remain unchanged.
Pneumonia	Extreme disappointment that an important opportunity has been missed, or fear one has made a large mistake.
Rash	Adverse reaction to a situation one feels powerless to change. *Who or what is irritating you?*
Sore Throat	*What can't you say? What can't you swallow or accept?*
Strep Throat	Stifling the truth for fear it may reflect poorly upon self and create trouble.
Tonsillitis	Always being told you are wrong and believing it, yet wishing it weren't true. Feeling uninvited and unwelcome.
Tuberculosis	Feeling at the mercy of those who are strong and in a position of power. "People are going to take things away."
UTI: Urinary Tract Infection	Anger (pissed-off) Unwilling or unable to express it; blaming.

Microbes

"Happiness and bacteria have one thing
in common; they multiply by dividing!"
— Rutvik Oza

Have you ever wondered why, in a classroom full of children exposed to the same bugs and germs, only a few get sick? Obviously, the condition of an individual's immune system--the body's natural ability to fight infection--and exposure to microscopic organisms that transmit disease, play a vital role. Surprisingly, a person's emotional state when exposed to these microbes can also influence whether or not he or she is an attractive "host" for these illnesses and/or diseases.

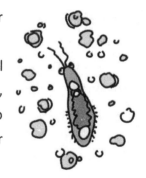

As we assess a child's physical symptoms, checking for fever, cough, or sore throat, we may want to address any negative feelings our child might be experiencing as well.

Microbes are attracted to specific negative emotions:

Bacteria	Attracted to feelings of guilt.
Viruses	Attracted to feelings of unworthiness.
Parasites	Indicate lack of boundaries somewhere. Feeling invaded or unsafe.
Fungus	Indicates something you want to hide or hide from; ugly thoughts and emotions that are eating at you.

When our child feels sick, we can seek to identify if he or she is struggling with feelings of guilt or unworthiness (feeling "not enough" in some area of life). These feelings are typically not generated by major incidents, but more likely from minor mistakes.

Applying the Emotional 911 sequence (Reveal, Release, Replace), we can invite our child to identify the person/incident/situation producing distress. By addressing the negative emotions involved, a child can shift to better feelings, removing blocks to the body's natural healing ability.

Once children know a physical symptom is simply a signal from their body, they begin to consider how the feelings they're having may be contributing to pain or illness. Wanting to feel better fast, a child is motivated to uncover emotional upsets he or she may have pushed under the proverbial rug.

With my own children, asking where they are feeling guilty, or "not good enough," has opened valuable discussions that otherwise may not have occurred. This works not only for children, but also adults.

Using a reported symptom as a clue, a typical exchange would go like this:

Child: Mom, my throat is sore and my chest hurts.
Me: Oh, I'm sorry to hear that. Is there anything you feel like you need to say to someone?
Child: I don't know.
Me: Okay. Is there anything you feel guilty about or somewhere you don't feel good enough?

Child: Well, maybe. Now that I think about it, I haven't told you and Dad that I got a "D" on my math test, and I guess I feel guilty I didn't study for it.

Me: That's a bummer. Thanks for telling me now. What's the worst part?

Child: I just didn't want you to be mad or disappoint you.

Me: I'll bet. So, what do you need to do to feel better?

Child: I already feel a little better from getting that off my chest. I don't want to feel bad like that again, so I'm going to make sure to keep up on my assignments during the next unit so it will be easier to study for the test.

Me: Good for you. Now, let's help your body feel better faster by imagining your body getting rid of those bad bugs, and replacing them with something better.

Of course, there may need to be follow-up conversations, additional support given, and perhaps, future consequences applied. However, staying solely in the role of "Validator"--not judge or jury--during this sequence a child feels safe to open up.

Validation helps clear distressing feelings to allow the body's natural healing wisdom to function.

Pac-Man

Use the Validation Hero Recipe or 3-step sequence of Emotional 911 to help a child **REVEAL** his or her upsetting emotions. Next, employ one of the best visualizations to **RELEASE and REPLACE** unwanted feelings, along with illness causing microbes. Suggest your child play an imaginary game of Pac-Man, the 1980's arcade pastime.

Invite your child to imagine the little ghosts as bad bugs, and the yellow Pac-Man as their immune system, gobbling up unwanted feelings and germs until  they are all devoured. Then, ask your child to imagine there are "goodies" (whatever a child wants to imagine those look like) that the Pac-Man can gulp down to be strong, healthy, and feel better.

Remember, after we release unwanted emotions we always want to intentionally replace them with something better.

Microbes play an important role for a healthy body and mind.

Once we've mended emotional causes of pain, the body responds quicker to physical remedies. Whether vitamins, minerals, or other supplements are needed, these become more effective when the body's natural healing wisdom is not emotionally compromised.

In addition, research is showing benefits received by replenishing the good bugs, or microorganisms in our body with probiotic supplements. Probiotics are comprised of multiple bacteria strains needed for healthy gut function. Studies have shown patients who received probiotics in clinical trials reported lower levels of depression and anxiety than patients who received placebos, due to the gut-brain connection (Microbes and the Mind, 2015).

Oobleck Recipe

1 cup water
1.5 - 2 cups cornstarch
(optional) - a few drops of food
coloring

Start with the water in a bowl and add about 1 cup of the cornstarch. If you are adding food coloring, do that now. Start by stirring with a spoon. Continue adding cornstarch. Once you've added 1.5 cups of the cornstarch, begin adding it in more slowly and mixing it in with your hand. The goal is to get to a consistency where the Oobleck reaches a state that is liquid and yet solid.

Sometimes, you will need to put in more cornstarch. If so, keep adding more than the initial 1.5 cups. If you add too much and it gets hard, just add more water into it. You will have to play with it to see what feels appropriately gloppy.

Tips:

- Oobleck isn't poisonous, but tastes awful.
- Store in an air-tight container. Mix occasionally.
- Adding food coloring might temporarily dye hands.
- Anything put into the slime can be washed clean with soap and water.
- To dispose of the Oobleck, mix with a lot of hot water making the goo into a loose slurry. Pour a small amount into the drain while the hot water is running.
- Oobleck, when dried, can be easily vacuumed.

(Sharp, 2012)

References

Ailes, R. w. (1988). *You Are the Message: Getting What You Want by Being Who You Are.* New York: Doubleday.

Baadsgaard, J. W. (1998, September). Mealtime, Family Time. *Ensign*, p. 22. Retrieved from https://www.lds.org/ensign/1998/09/mealtime-family-time?lang=eng

Babbel, S. P. (2010, Apr 8). The Connections Between Emotional Stress, Trauma and Physical Pain. Retrieved from https://www.psychologytoday.com/us/blog/somatic-psychology/201004/the-connections-between-emotional-stress-trauma-and-physical-pain

Book, L. (n.d.). Retrieved August 23, 2018, from https://laurenskids.org/

Bowlby, J. (1969). *Attachment and Loss: Vol 1. Attachment.* New York: Basic Books.

Brooks, A. W. (2014, June). Get Excited: Reappraising Pre-Performance Anxiety as Excitement. *Journal of Experiemental Psychology, General 143*(3), 1144-1158. Retrieved from https://www.hbs.edu/faculty/Pages/item.aspx?num=45869

Brown, B. P. (2010). *The Gifts of Imperfection: Let Go of Who You Think You're Supposed to Be and Embrace Who You Are.* Center City: Hazelden.

Burmeister, M. (1988). *Fun With Happy Hands.* Retrieved September 5, 2018, from https://www.jsjinc.net/proddetail.php?prod=HH

Cline, F. M. (2006). *Parenting with Love and Logic:.* Colorado Springs: NavPress. Retrieved from www.loveandlogic.com

Cole, M. &. (1994). The development of emotional regulation and dysregulations: A clinical perspective. *Monographs of the Society for Research in Child Development. Vol 59*, 73-100.

Collins, L. (2017, Dec 19). This is what helping strangers can do for your teen, according to a new BYU study. *Deseret News.* Retrieved from https://www.deseretnews.com/article/900005985/this-is-what-helping-strangers-can-do-for-your-teen-according-to-a-new-byu-study.html

Conrad, B. D. (n.d.). Addiction to Video Games - 6 Common Problems To Watch For. *Tech Addiction*. Retrieved September 20, 2018, from http://www.techaddiction.ca/addiction-to-video-games.html

Cuddy, A. (2012). Your Body Language Shapes Who You Are. *TEDGlobal*. Retrieved from https://www.ted.com/talks/amy_cuddy_your_body_language_shapes_who_you_are/transcript

Curran, T. a. (2018, Jan 5). The rise of perfectionism is negatively affecting young people. *World Economic Forum*. Retrieved from https://www.weforum.org/agenda/2018/01/perfectionism-has-become-a-hidden-epidemic-amoung-young-people

Damour, L. P. (2016). *Untangled: Guiding Teenage Girls Through the Seven Transitions Into Adulthood.* New York: Ballantine Books.

DeSalvo, L. (1999). *Writing as a Way of Healing.* Boston: Beacon Press.

Dobbs, B. (2015). In B. Dobbs, *When Hope Is Not Enough: A How-To Guide For Living With and Loving Someone with Borderline Personality Disorder* (pp. 103-104). Dobbs, Bon. Retrieved from http://www.anythingtostopthepain.com/validating-statement-revealed/

Duckworth, A. (2016). *Grit: The Power of Passion and Perseverance.* New York: Simon & Schuster.

Dweck, C. S. (2006). *Mindset: The Psychology of Success.* New York: Ballantine Books.

Emmons, R. A. (2003, Feb). Counting blessings in adolescents: An experiemental study of gratitude and subjective well-being in daily life. *Journal of Personality and Social Psychology*, pp. 213-33.

Emoto, M. (2010). The Power of Love and Gratitude Made Visible. (L. Images used by permission Office Masaru Emoto, Ed.) Retrieved from http://www.masaru-emoto.net/english/water-crystal.html

Fahad, B. D. (2015, Dec 3). 11 Benefits of Hugging - Back by Chemistry. Retrieved from https://www.collective-evolution.com/2015/12/03/the-chemistry-of-hugging-11-benefits-of-hugging/

Fields, K. (2017, December 17). Life in Balance: What children are doing on their cell phones. *KTVB.com*. Retrieved from https://www.ktvb.com/article/life/life-in-balance/life-in-balance-what-children-are-doing-on-their-cell-phones/277-500203220

Fox, K. (2017, May 19). Instagram worst social media app for young people's mental health. *CNN*. Retrieved from https://www.cnn.com/2017/05/19/health/instagram-worst-social-network-app-young-people-mental-health/index.html

Gilbert, D. T. (1993). You can't not believe everything you read. *Journal of Personality and Social Psychology*, pp. 65, 221-233.

Graham, J. (2018, July 5). When a child is traumatized, this one thing helps their recovery the most. *Deseret News*. Retrieved from https://www.deseretnews.com/article/900023789/when-a-child-is-traumatized-this-one-thing-helps-their-recovery-the-most.html

Grahame-Smith, S. (. (n.d.). *The Lego Batman Movie*. Warner Animation Group. Retrieved from http://www.legobatman.com/

Hadhazy, A. (2010, Feb 12). Think Twice: How the Gut's "Second Brain" Influences Mood and Well-Being. *Scientific American*. Retrieved from https://www.scientificamerican.com/article/gut-second-brain/

Hankin, A. M. (1998). Development of depression from preadolescence to young adulthood: Emerging gender differences in a 10-year longitudinal study. *Journal of Abnormal Psychology*, 107: 128-140.

Harris, B. D. (2015). *Trails to Testimony.* Harris, Bradley D.

Heid, M. (2017, Aug 2). You Asked: Is Social Media Making Me Miserable? *TIME Magazine*. Retrieved from http://time.com/4882372/social-media-facebook-instagram-unhappy/

Hendrickson, E. ". (2016, Jan 27). Should Kids Take Psychiatric Medication? *Scientific American*. Retrieved from https://www.scientificamerican.com/article/should-kids-take-psychiatric-medication/

Hurley, D. (2013, May). Grandma's Experiences Leave a Mark on Your Genes. *Discover Magazine*. Retrieved from http://discovermagazine.com/2013/may/13-grandmas-experiences-leave-epigenetic-mark-on-your-genes

Johnson, S. a. (2016). *Created for Connection: The "Hold Me Tight" Guide for Christian Couples*. Little, Brown.

Justice, T. U. (n.d.). Raising Awareness About Sexual Abuse: Facts and Statistics. *NSOPW*, p. Education and Prevention. Retrieved August 2018, from https://www.nsopw.gov/(X(1)S(tb1s0jeckf2jr1lryravm1ej))/en/Education/FactsStatistics?AspxAutoDetectCookieSupport=1

Kanwisher, N. (2000, Nov 1). Seeing and imagining are the same to the brain, MIT research shows. *MIT News*. Retrieved from http://news.mit.edu/2000/mindseye

Kircher-Morris, E. L. (2015, Dec 7). Why 'Toughen Up' Doesn't Cut It with Children and Teens. Retrieved from https://www.goodtherapy.org/blog/why-toughen-up-doesnt-cut-it-with-children-and-teens-1207155

Kubler-Ross, E. a. (2000). *Life Lessons: Two Experts on Death and Dying Teach Us About the Mysteries of Life and Living*. New York: Scribner.

Lane, C. P. (2010, Sep 2). Medicating Children: The Controversy over "Early Detection". *Psychology Today*. Retrieved from https://www.psychologytoday.com/us/blog/side-effects/201009/medicating-children-the-controversy-over-early-detection

Lerner, C. (2017, Feb 17). Babies and Stress: The Facts. *Zero To Three Organization*. Retrieved from https://www.zerotothree.org/resources/1709-babies-and-stress-the-facts

M, A. (2017, Oct 16). Top 10 Simple Brain Gym Exercises And Its Benefits. *Stylecraze*. Retrieved from https://www.stylecraze.com/articles/simple-brain-gym-exercises-and-its-benefits/#gref

Macnamara, B. N. (2014, July 1). Deliberate Practice and Performance in Music, Games, Sports, Education, and Professions: A Meta-Analysis. *Psychological Science Online First*. Retrieved from https://scottbarrykaufman.com/wp-content/uploads/2014/07/Macnamara-et-al.-2014.pdf

Mastin, L. (2018). Episodic and Semantic Memory. Retrieved from http://www.human-memory.net/types_episodic.html

McBeath, S. A. (1999-2018). Making Change in Our Lives. *Physical Conditions and Their Spiritual Components* retrieved November 1, 2018, from www.ourspiritualnutrition.com

Microbes and the Mind. (2015, August 25). *Neuroscientifically Challenged.* Retrieved August 23, 2018, from https://www.neuroscientificallychallenged.com/blog/micro bes-and-the-mind

Mischel, W. (2014). *The Marshmallow Test: Why Self Control is the Engine of Success.* New York, Boston, London: Little, Brown and Company.

Morrissey, M. (2016, Sep 14). The Power of Writing Down Your Goals and Dreams. *Huffington Post.* Retrieved Sep. 2018, from https://www.huffingtonpost.com/marymorrissey/the-power-of-writing-down_b_12002348.html

Nelson, J. E. (2006). *Positive Discipline: The Classic Guide to Helping Children Develop Self-Discipline, Responsibility, Cooperation, and Problem-Solving Skills.* New York: Ballantine Books.

Newberg, A. a. (2012). *Words Can Change Your Brain: 12 Conversation Strategies to Build Trust, Resolve Conflict, and Increase Intimacy.* New York: Penguin Group.

Northrup, C. (2006). *Women's Bodies, Women's Wisdom.* New York: Bantam Dell.

Northrup, C. (2006). *Women's Bodies, Women's Wisdom: Creating Physical and Emotional Health.* New York: Bantam Dell.

Nott, L. (2013, Jul 2). Teens Are Feeling More Anxious Than Ever. *Elements Behavioral Health.* Retrieved September 2018, from https://www.elementsbehavioralhealth.com/featured/teen agers-are-feeling-more-anxious-than-ever/

Ollendick, T. a. (1990). Depression in British and American children and its relation to anxiety and fear. *Journal of Consulting and Clinical Psychology,* 58: 126-129.

Pascual-Leone Nguyet, C. B.-N. (1995). *Modulation of muscle responses evoked by transcranial magnetic stimulation during the acquisition of new fine motor skills.* Retrieved from https://www.ncbi.nlm.nih.gov/pubmed/7500130

Prior, V. a. (2006). *Understanding Attachment and Attachment Disorders: Theory, Evidence and Practice.* London and Philadelphia: Jessica Kingsley.

Remen, R. N. (1996). *Kitchen Table Wisdom Stories That Heal.* New York: Berkley Publishing Group.

Rosenfeld, J. (2018, April 11). 11 Scientific Benefits of Having a Laugh. *Mental Floss.* Retrieved September 2018, from http://mentalfloss.com/article/539632/scientific-benefits-having-laugh

Russo, F. B. (2015, April 17). Duracell Canada Moments of Warmth surprise bus shelter. p. https://youtu.be/yGxRLrjc7Z0.

Satir, V. (2014, Jan 23). 9 Reasons You Need To Be Giving and Receiving Hugs Everyday. *Prevent Disease.*

Sea, A. (n.d.). Somatic Trauma Resolution. Retrieved July 7, 2018, from http://www.andreasea.com/somatic_trauma_resolution.html

Seery, M. D. (2010). Whatever Does Not Kill Us: Cumulative Lifetime Adversity, Vulnerability, and Resilience. *Journal of Personality and Society Psychology, 99*(6), 1025-1041. Retrieved from https://webfiles.uci.edu/rsilver/Seery,%20Holman,%20&%20Silver%202010%20JPSP.pdf

Sharp, T. (2012, July 11). How to Make Oobleck. *Live Science.* Retrieved from https://www.livescience.com/21536-oobleck-recipe.html

Siegel, R. A. (2017, May). The Power of Fake Pills. *Smithsonian Institution.*

Simmons, M. (2017, Oct 26). Forget the 10,000 Hour Rule; Edison, Bezos, & Zuckerberg Follow The 10,000-Experiment Rule. *Medium.* Retrieved from https://medium.com/@michaeldsimmons/forget-about-the-10-000-hour-rule-7b7a39343523

Simpson, J. a. (1998). *Attachment Theory and Close Relationships.* New York: The Guilford Press.

Snyder, H. N. (2000). *Sexual Assault of Young Children as Reported to Law Enforcement.* National Center for Juvenile Justice.

Steiner, C. w. (1997). *Achieving Emotional Literacy.* London: Bloomsbury.

Twenge, J. M. (2017). *iGen: Why Today's Super-Connected Kids Are Growing Up Less Rebellious, More Tolerant, Less Happy-- and Completely Unprepared for Adulthood--and What That Means for the Rest of Us.* Simon & Shuster.

Uchtdorf, D. F. (2017, May). Pefect Love Casteth Out Fear. *Ensign*, pp. 104-107.

Verrier, N. N. (1993). *The Primal Wound.* Baltimore: Gateway Press.

Wilson, D. (2010, September 1). Child's Ordeal Shows Risks of Psychosis Drugs for Young. *New York Times*. Retrieved from https://www.nytimes.com/2010/09/02/business/02kids.ht ml

Wong, D. (2014, Dec 24). 7 phrases that children need to hear from their parents. *Huffington Post*. Retrieved from https://www.huffingtonpost.com/daniel-wong/7-phrases-that-children-n_b_6039804.html

Yerkovich, M. a. (2017). *How We Love: Discover Your Love Style, Improve Your Marriage.* Colorado Springs: Alive Communications.

Meet the Author

Laura Sonderegger delights in sunshine, singing, sharing and smiles. A four-season outdoor enthusiast with her adventurous husband, three children, and their two newlywed spouses, Laura lives for beach days and boating. Ever hosting gatherings, Laura enjoys bringing people together and connecting one-on-one. Her superpowers are "heart healer" and "monster cookie" maker.

An expert in emotional epigenetic reprogramming, Laura integrates the best and most effective techniques from her training in a host of healing modalities, including: Neuro-Linguistic Programming (NLP), Energy Freedom Technique (EFT), Reference Point Therapy (RPT), Energy Medicine, Positive Psychology, and other healing arts. Offering fast and lasting relief, Laura guides both children and adults to overcome past trauma and mend present drama.

Laura transforms lives through a thriving private practice in Meridian, Idaho, as well as an extensive coast-to-coast phone or Skype session service. A sought-after speaker, teacher and health facilitator, Laura inspires others to clear their blocks and attain desired goals.

In this book, Laura shares her 3-step sequence of EMOTIONAL 911 which teaches how to: *reveal* unhealthy emotions and broken beliefs manifesting as emotional or physical discomfort; *release* limiting feelings, beliefs, or programs, and *replace* with positive, powerful feelings, activating the body's ability to **heal from the inside out**.

Dear Reader,

If you have found this book a valuable parenting resource would you please go to Amazon and leave a positive review?

Amazon uses reviews to rank books and many readers evaluate the quality of a title based solely on the feedback from others.

Even a sentence or two about what you like really helps. I appreciate your support!

Thanks! Laura